WordPress 2.7 Complete

Create your own complete blog or website from scratch
with WordPress

April Hodge Silver

Hasin Hayder

PUBLISHING

BIRMINGHAM - MUMBAI

WordPress 2.7 Complete

First published: May 2009

Production Reference: 2040609

Published by Packt Publishing Ltd.
32 Lincoln Road
Olton
Birmingham, B27 6PA, UK.

ISBN 978-1-847196-56-9

www.packtpub.com

Cover Image by Parag Kadam (paragvkadam@gmail.com)

Credits

Authors

April Hodge Silver

Hasin Hayder

Reviewers

Lee Jordan

Narayan Bhat

Paul Thewlis

Acquisition Editor

David Barnes

Development Editor

Ved Prakash Jha

Technical Editor

Reshma Sundaresan

Copy Editor

Sneha Kulkarni

Editorial Team Leader

Abhijeet Deobhakta

Project Team Leader

Lata Basantani

Project Coordinator

Leena Purkait

Indexer

Rekha Nair

Proofreader

Sandra Hopper

Production Coordinator

Shantanu Zagade

Cover Work

Shantanu Zagade

About the authors

April Hodge Silver has been designing and developing new websites from scratch since 1999, just before her graduation from Columbia University. Early in her career, she worked for several web companies and startups, including DoubleClick and About.com. Since 2004, she has been self-employed through her company Springthistle Design and has worked with a staggering variety of companies, non-profits, and individuals to realize their website dreams. In her professional work, April's focus is always on usability, efficiency, flexibility, clean design, and client happiness. WordPress is the best solution for many of Springthistle's clients, though April also develops custom web applications using PHP and MySQL. You can find out more about April's professional work at `http://springthistle.com`.

In her free time, April enjoys developing recipes in the kitchen, bicycling, and relaxing with her daughter, dog, and darlin' wife.

Of course, I am so grateful to everyone at Packt who worked with me to make this book possible. Also, a huge bunch of thanks to my wife Tessa, who made the connection in the first place and helped me get started in this medium. Finally, thanks go to Ruth and Hazel, who provided guidance on commas.

Hasin Hayder graduated in Civil Engineering from the Rajshahi University of Engineering and Technology (RUET) in Bangladesh. He is a Zend-certified Engineer and expert in developing localized applications. He is currently working as a Technical Director in Trippert Labs and managing the local branch in Bangladesh. Beside his full time job, Hasin writes his blog at http://hasin.wordpress.com, writes article in different websites and maintains his open source framework Orchid at http://orchid.phpxperts.net. Hasin lives in Bangladesh with his wife Ayesha and his son, Afif.

First of all, I would like to thank David Barnes, Patricia Weir, Abhijeet Deobhakta, and Nikhil Bangera, without whom the book would have never seen the daylight. After writing for so many sleepless nights, the book is finally over; but I want to thank all those who supported me at that time. My wife Ayesha for storytelling, Little Afif for missing his Papa, the staff of Somewhere In for receiving a sleepy developer in the morning, the staff of Pageflakes for their inspiration, and all the members of my PHP group, phpexperts. I would also like to thank all my family members for their great support during this period. Finally, I dedicate this book to the person who would have been the happiest person to see it; my father, Ali Akbar Mohammad Mohiuddin Hayder (1934-2006).

About the reviewers

Lee Jordan is a web developer with a large collection of web technology acronyms on her resume that sound like the names of laundry detergents and cause glazed expressions in school children. She designs and maintains internal and external enterprise-level websites and web-based applications as part of a project team for a privately held technical services company. Her work includes proposing, writing, and editing web content and user guides people actually read. She began her career in 1997 as a web designer after graduating from Florida State University with a Bachelor of Fine Arts, where she swears that she missed at least one home football game while in the computer lab. Lee later convinced Seminole Community College to give her a Web Programming degree in 2003 even though her final project was a Java-based application that actually contained a usable help file.

Web development topics or whatever she can think of at the time are posted on her blog at `http://leejordan.net`.

Narayan Bhat's current passion is blogging. You can meet him at his site: The Blog Doctor (`http://www.blogdoctor.me`).

He has reviewed *Blogger Beyond the Basics* and *WordPress for Business Bloggers*, both by Packt Publishing.

Paul Thewlis has worked as a web communications professional in the public and private sectors. He is currently E-Communications Manager for a multinational transport company headquartered in the UK. He began his web career as a Technical Editor, working on web design books for a well-known publisher. He has extensive experience of many content management systems and blogging platforms. He is an expert in the use of social media within corporate communications and blogs about that subject, as well as WordPress and the Web in general at `http://blog.paulthewlis.com`.

Paul is the author of *WordPress For Business Bloggers*, also by Packt Publishing

Table of Contents

Preface

Using WordPress, you can easily create dynamic blogs and websites with great content and many outstanding features. It is an ideal tool for developing blogs and though it is chiefly used for blogging, it can also be used as a complete CMS for a regular website with very little effort. You can customize the features, incorporate your own design, and even write your own plugins with ease. Its versatility and ease of use has attracted a large, enthusiastic, and helpful community of users. Although it is easy to get started with WordPress, its full power is not immediately obvious.

If you want to create a powerful, fully featured blog or non-blog website in no time, this book is for you. This book will help you learn everything WordPress has to offer from the ground up, so you can build your complete website. You will see many of WordPress's hidden powers that will help you build a fully functioning website.

What this book covers

Chapter 1 – Introduction to WordPress introduces everything about blogging, including what a blog is, the common terms used in blogging and what they mean, what WordPress has to offer to a blogger, and why to choose it.

Chapter 2 – Getting Started explains the choices of where you can build your WordPress website, upgrading from an older version of WordPress, and getting familiar with the WordPress Administration Panel.

Chapter 3 – Blogging Your Heart Out covers the complete process of creating new posts for your blog, including applying categories and tags to your post, using the rich text editor, and controlling the timestamp. It also includes more advanced options such as including excerpt and trackbacks. This chapter also covers controlling commenting and discussion on your blog, as well as keeping out comment spam.

Chapter 4 – Pages, Images, Plugins and More... explains that blog posts aren't the only content in your blog. You also can control pages of static information, upload and manage images on your site, keep a list of bookmarked links, and add plugins.

Chapter 5 – Choosing and Installing Themes covers how to find and use existing themes from a variety of reliable websites, how to choose which theme is right for your website or blog, and the process of installing and using your new theme. This chapter also covers enabling and using widgets in your theme.

Chapter 6 – Developing Your Own Theme covers the process of creating your own theme from soup to nuts. This includes setting up your design to accommodate your blogging goals, converting your initial build into an authentic WordPress theme, creating templates within your theme to serve different purposes for your blog, making your theme widget-friendly, and sharing your theme with the WordPress community.

Chapter 7 – Feeds and Podcasting explains what feeds are and how to add them to your WordPress website, tracking subscribers to your blog, and aggregating feeds from other sources on your blog. This chapter also covers using your WordPress website to create a podcast. (It's easy!)

Chapter 8 – Developing Plugins and Widgets is for the more advanced user. This chapter shows you how to create plugins and widgets that will work with any installation of WordPress. It includes step-by-step instructions so you don't get lost along the way.

Chapter 9 – Community Blogging covers managing and handling a multiuser blog, including a detailed outline of the roles and capabilities included in WordPress.

Chapter 10 – WordPress as a CMS covers from start to finish how to use WordPress to create a non-blog website. This chapter includes explanations of designing your theme, setting it up, creating custom pages that display post content in non-blog ways, customizing the home page to contain dynamic content, and creating a news page.

Chapter11 – Administrator's Reference covers all of the basic things a WordPress administrator needs to know from system requirements to detailed step-by-step instructions on installing WordPress, moving your WordPress website from one place to another, backing up, common template tags, and basic troubleshooting.

What you need for this book

The minimum system requirement for WordPress is a web server with the following software installed:

- PHP Version 4.3 or greater
- MySQL Version 4.0 or greater

Who this book is for

This book is a guide to WordPress for both beginners and progressive learners. It's for people who are new to blogging and want to create their own blogs in a simple and straightforward manner, and it's also for those who want to learn how to customize and expand the capabilities of a WordPress website.

It does not require any detailed knowledge of programming or web development, and any IT-confident user will be able to use the book to produce an impressive blog.

Conventions

In this book, you will find a number of styles of text that distinguish between different kinds of information. Here are some examples of these styles, and an explanation of their meaning.

Code words in text are shown as follows: "...you can add the above text anywhere in `single.php` so long as it is inside the `if` and `while` loops of the *loop*."

A block of code will be set as follows:

```
function modify_menu_for_supportedtypes() {
    add_management_page(
        'Document Types', // Page <title>
        'Document Types', // Menu title
        7,                // What level of user
        __FILE__,             //File to open
        'supportedtypes_options'  //Function to call
        );
}
```

When we wish to draw your attention to a particular part of a code block, the relevant lines or items will be shown in bold:

```
<h1>
    <a href="<?php echo get_option('home'); ?>/">
        <?php bloginfo('name'); ?></a>
</h1>
<div id="description"><?php bloginfo('description'); ?></div>
```

Any command-line input or output is written as follows:

```
chmod -R wp-admin 744
```

New terms and **important words** are shown in bold. Words that you see on the screen, in menus or dialog boxes for example, appear in our text like this: "To register your free blog, click on the loud blue-and-white **Sign Up Now!** button."

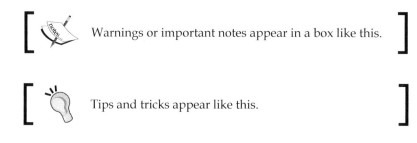

Warnings or important notes appear in a box like this.

Tips and tricks appear like this.

Reader feedback

Feedback from our readers is always welcome. Let us know what you think about this book—what you liked or may have disliked. Reader feedback is important for us to develop titles that you really get the most out of.

To send us general feedback, simply drop an email to feedback@packtpub.com, and mention the book title in the subject of your message.

If there is a book that you need and would like to see us publish, please send us a note in the **SUGGEST A TITLE** form on www.packtpub.com or email suggest@packtpub.com.

If there is a topic that you have expertise in and you.are interested in either writing or contributing to a book, see our author guide on www.packtpub.com/authors.

Customer support

Now that you are the proud owner of a Packt book, we have a number of things to help you to get the most from your purchase.

Downloading the example code for the book

Visit http://www.packtpub.com/files/code/6569_Code.zip to directly download the example code.

The downloadable files contain instructions on how to use them.

Errata

Although we have taken every care to ensure the accuracy of our contents, mistakes do happen. If you find a mistake in one of our books—maybe a mistake in text or code—we would be grateful if you would report this to us. By doing so, you can save other readers from frustration and help us to improve subsequent versions of this book. If you find any errata, please report them by visiting http://www.packtpub.com/support, selecting your book, clicking on the **let us know** link, and entering the details of your errata. Once your errata are verified, your submission will be accepted and the errata added to any list of existing errata. Any existing errata can be viewed by selecting your title from http://www.packtpub.com/support.

Piracy

Piracy of copyright material on the Internet is an ongoing problem across all media. At Packt, we take the protection of our copyright and licenses very seriously. If you come across any illegal copies of our works in any form on the Internet, please provide us with the location address or website name immediately so that we can pursue a remedy.

Please contact us at copyright@packtpub.com with a link to the suspected pirated material.

We appreciate your help in protecting our authors, and our ability to bring you valuable content.

Questions

You can contact us at questions@packtpub.com if you are having a problem with any aspect of the book, and we will do our best to address it.

1
Introduction to WordPress

These days, everyone can find a reason for having a website. It's not just the large companies who have a website. Even individuals, families, and small or independent businesses need to have one. Some individuals and small businesses do not have the financial resources to hire a website development company to create a website for them. This is where WordPress comes in. WordPress is a web application that you can use to create and maintain an online website, even if you have a minimum of technical expertise.

Because it is a web application, WordPress does not need to be installed on your home computer. It can live on the computer that belongs to your website hosting company. It is also free, easy to use, and packed with excellent features. Originally, WordPress was an application meant to run a blog website, but it has now evolved into a fully-featured **Content Management System (CMS)**.

In this chapter, we'll explore the characteristics of a blog, the most essential terminologies used in blogging, the greatest advantages of WordPress (that is, why you should choose it), and online resources for WordPress.

What is a blog?

A **blog**, which is short for **weblog**, is a website that usually contains regular entries like any other kind of log. These entries can be of various types such as commentary, descriptions of events, photos, videos, personal remarks, or political ideas. They are usually displayed in reverse chronological order, with the most recent additions on the top. These entries can be organized in a variety of ways—by date, by topic, by subject, and so on.

A blog is a special type of website that gets updated regularly. Unlike a site where the content is static, a blog behaves more like an online diary wherein the blogger posts regular updates. Hence, blogs are dynamic with ever-changing content. A blog can be updated with new content and the old content can be changed or deleted at any time.

Most blogs focus their content on a particular subject—for example current events, hobbies, technical expertise—or else they are more like personal online diaries.

According to Wikipedia, the term *weblog* was first used in 1997 and people started using blogs globally in 1999. The terms *weblog*, *weblogging*, and *weblogger* were added to the Oxford Dictionary in 2003, though these days most people leave off the "we" part at the front.

Common terms

If you are new to the world of blogging, you may want to familiarize yourself with these common terminologies.

Post

Each entry in the blog is called a **post**. Every post usually has a number of different parts. Of course, the two most obvious parts are title and content. The **content** is text, images, links, and so on. Posts can even contain multimedia. Every post also has a publication timestamp, and most also have one or more categories, tags, comments, and so on. It is these posts, or entries, that are displayed in a reverse chronological order on the main page of the blog. The latest post is displayed first in order to give the viewer the latest news on the subject.

Categories and tags

Categories and **tags** are ways to organize and find posts within a blog and even across blogs. Categories are like topics, whereas tags are more like keywords. For example, for a blog about food and cooking, there might be a category called **Recipes**, but every post in that category would have different tags (for example, soup, baked, vegetarian, dairy-free, and so on).

Comments

Most blogs allow visitors to post comments about the posts. This gives readers the opportunity to interact with the writer of the blog, thus making the whole enterprise interactive. Often, the writer of the blog will respond to comments by posting comments, which makes for a continuous public online conversation or dialogue.

Permalinks

A blog has dozens or hundreds of posts, each of which has a unique ID, and so, many blog engines provide a way to link directly to each post. A **permalink** is a nicely-formatted link that usually has some form of the post title in the link. For example, a post with the title **Everything You Wanted To Know About Eggplant** might have the permalink `http://myblog.com/everything-you-wanted-to-know-about-eggplant`. Permalinks are often more search-engine-friendly, especially if the blogger keeps search engines in mind when creating titles.

Permalinks is WordPress's fancy word for what used to be called SEO-friendly URLs. **SEO** stands for **Search Engine Optimization** because sensible URLs, like permalinks, are easier for search engines (such as Google and Yahoo) to catalog. These days, they are often known as *pretty* or *user-friendly* URLs. These URLs tell a story about the page they represent, and don't have a lot of confusing punctuations in them. For example, if you are looking at a blog archive for the month of April 2008 in WordPress, the regular URL would look like this: `http://yoursite.com/index.php?m=200804`. If you enable permalinks, the URL will look like this instead: `http://yoursite.com/2008/04/post_title/`. An even bigger contrast shows up if you're looking at pages. Let's say you have a page with information about you, the author of your blog. The regular URL would look like this: `http://yoursite.com/index.php?page_id=23`. If you enable permalinks, the URL will look like this: `http://yoursite.com/about`.

Theme

The **theme** for a blog is the design and layout that you choose for your blog. In most blogs, the content (for example, posts) is separate from the visual layout. This means you can change the visual layout of your blog at any time without having to worry about the content being affected.

RSS

RSS is an acronym for **Really Simple Syndication**, and Chapter 7 addresses the topic of feeds in detail. For now, understand that RSS and feeds are a way to syndicate the content of your blog so that people can subscribe to it. This means people do not actually have to visit your blog regularly to see what you've added. They can subscribe and have new content delivered to them via email or through a feed reader.

Page

It's important to understand the difference between a page and a post. Unlike posts, pages do not depend on having timestamps and are not displayed in chronological order. They also do not have categories or tags. A **page** is a piece of content with only a title and content (an example would be **About Me** or **Contact Us**). It is likely that the number of pages on your site remains relatively static, whereas new posts are added every day or so. Thus pages have static content, while posts have dynamic content.

What is WordPress?

WordPress is an open source blog engine. **Open source** means that nobody owns it, everybody works on it, and anyone can contribute to it. **Blog engine** means a software that can run a blog. It's a piece of software that lives on the web server and makes it easy for you to add and edit posts, themes, comments, and all of your other content. More expansively, WordPress can be called a *publishing platform* because it is by no means restricted to blogging.

WordPress was originally a fork of an older piece of software called *b2/cafelog*. WordPress was developed by Matt Mullenweg and Mike Little, but is now maintained and developed by a team of developers that includes Mullenweg.

Why choose WordPress?

WordPress is not the only publishing platform out there, but it has an awful lot to recommend it. In the following sections, I've called attention to WordPress's most outstanding features.

A long time in refining

In web years, WordPress has been around for quite a while and was in development the whole time, getting better constantly. WordPress's very first release, Version 0.70, was released in May 2003. Since then, it has had nine major releases, with a number of minor ones in between. Each release came with more features and better security.

Active in development

WordPress is a constantly evolving application. It's never left alone to stagnate. The developers are working continually to keep it ahead of spammers and hackers, and also to evolve the application based on the evolving needs of its users.

Large community of contributors

WordPress is not being developed by a lonely programmer in a dark basement room. On the contrary, there is a large community of people working on it by developing, troubleshooting, making suggestions, and testing the application. With such a large group of people involved, the application is most likely to have continued well-being.

Amazingly extendable

In addition to having an extremely strong core, WordPress is also quite extendable. This means that once you get started with it, the possibilities are nearly limitless. Any additional functionality that you can dream of can be added by way of a plugin that you or your programmer friends can write.

Detailed feature list

Here is a detailed list of many features of WordPress:

- All standards are compliant with W3C
- Unlimited categories and subcategories
- Automatic syndication (RSS and Atom)
- Uses XML RPC interface for trackbacks and remote posting
- Allows posting via email
- Supports plugins and themes
- Imports data from other blogs (Moveable Type, Textpattern, Greymatter, b2evolution, and blogger)
- Easy to administer and blog without any previous experience
- Convenient, fully functional, built-in search
- Instant and fast publishing of content—no re-building of pages required
- Multilanguage capable
- Link manager
- Allows password-protected posts
- Comments manager and spam protection
- Built-in workflow (write, draft, review, and publish)
- Intelligent text formatting

Learning more

You can read a fully explained feature list at `http://wordpress.org/about/features/`.

Online WordPress resources

One very useful characteristic of WordPress is that it has a large, active online community. Everything you will ever need for your WordPress website can be found online, and probably for free.

WordPress news

As WordPress is always actively developed, it's important to keep yourself up-to-date with the software community about their latest activities. The most important spot to visit or subscribe to is WordPress Releases: `http://wordpress.org/development/category/releases/`. Whenever there is a new release—be it a major release, or an interim bug fix, or an upgrade—it will be here.

Learning more

Also, be sure to stay tuned to the main WordPress blog at `http://wordpress.org/development/`.

The Codex

The WordPress **Codex** is the central repository of all the information the official WordPress team has published to help people work with WordPress.

The Codex has some basic tutorials for getting started with WordPress such as a detailed step-by-step discussion of installation, lists of every template tag and hook, and a lot more. Throughout this book, I'll be providing links to specific pages within the Codex, which will provide more or advanced information on the topics in this book.

Theme and plugin directories

There are official directories for themes and for plugins on wordpress.org. Though not every theme and plugin is available here, the ones that are here have been vetted by the community to some extent. Anything you download from these directories is likely to be relatively bug-free. You can also see what the community thinks of these downloads by looking at ratings, comments, and popularity.

Additionally, plugins in the **Plugin Directory** are automatically upgradable from within your WordPress Administration Panel, whereas other plugins have to be upgraded manually.

Theme Directory: http://wordpress.org/extend/themes/

Plugin Directory: http://wordpress.org/extend/plugins/

WordPress.com

You'll notice that all of the URLs above belong to wordpress.org. There is another website, wordpress.com, which is actually a free blog-hosting service. Anyone can open an account on WordPress.com and instantly have his or her own WordPress-driven blog. According to WordPress.com, there were over 6 million blogs on WordPress.com and over 9 million active installations of the WordPress.org software as of December 2008.

In Chapter 2, we will discuss all of the differences between having your blog on WordPress.com versus downloading the software from wordpress.org and hosting it yourself, but the basic difference is the level of control. If your blog is on WordPress.com, you have less control over plugins, themes, and other details of the blog because everything is managed and made worry-free by the WordPress.com service.

Summary

Blogging is a wonderful pastime for just about anyone who has something interesting to say, and WordPress is excellent software that can run your blog (or non-blog) website. It's packed with excellent features and is so flexible that it can really do anything you want. Additionally, it's super easy to use, and you need no special skills or prior experience to use it. Last but not the least, it is free!

In this chapter, we learned about blogging and common blog terms. We also looked into the reasons to choose WordPress for blogging and the online resources available for WordPress users. In the next chapter, we will explore the choices and steps involved in installing WordPress.

2
Getting Started

This chapter will guide you through the process of setting up WordPress and customizing its basic features. WordPress is relatively smaller (only 1.2 MB), easier to install, and easier to administer. This chapter will show you the different options for installing WordPress and setting it up.

WordPress is available in easily downloadable formats from its website at `http://wordpress.org/download/`. Currently, WordPress Version 2.7.1 is available for download. WordPress is a free, open source application, and is released under the GNU **General Public License (GPL)**. Anyone who produces a modified version of software released under the GPL is required to keep those same freedoms attached to his or her modified version. This way, WordPress and other software released under GPL are kept free and open source.

There is a slightly different version of WordPress that is capable of supporting multiuser blogging. This means several users can maintain separate blogs within a single installation of WordPress. They can log into and maintain their blogs independently of one another. This version of WordPress is known as **WordPress MU** or **WordPress Multi-User**. In this book, we will only cover the installation and use of WordPress.

In this chapter, you will learn how to:

- Create a free blog on WordPress.com
- Install WordPress manually on your web host
- Upgrade WordPress from an older installation
- Perform basic setup tasks in the WordPress Admin panel

Where to build your WordPress website

The first decision you have to make is where your blog is going to live. You have two basic options for the location where you can create (or build) your site. They are:

- Build on WordPress.com
- Build on your own server

The advantage of building on WordPress.com is that they take care of all of the technical details for you. The software is already installed; they'll upgrade it for you whenever there's an upgrade, and you're not responsible for anything else. The big disadvantage is that you lose almost all of the theme and plugin control you'd have otherwise. WordPress.com will not let you upload or edit your own theme, and will only let you edit the CSS of your theme if you pay a fee ($15/year currently). WordPress.com will not let you upload or manage plugins at all. Some plugins are installed by default (most notably Akismet, for spam blocking and a fancy statistics plugin), but you can neither uninstall them nor install others. This chapter will cover creating a blog on WordPress.com, and you can learn about navigating around the WP Admin in the next chapter. However, much of what this book covers will be impossible on WordPress.com.

The huge advantage of building on your own server (which probably means a server that belongs to the web host that you signed up with) is that you have control over everything. You can add and edit themes, add and remove plugins, and even edit the WordPress application files yourself. You'll have to keep your own WordPress software up-to-date, but that's relatively simple and we'll cover it in this chapter.

As I said, we'll discuss building on WordPress.com in this chapter. But you will have to build on your own server if you want to accomplish any of the more advanced topics from this book.

The following table is a brief overview of the essential differences between building on WordPress.com versus your own server:

	WordPress.com	Your Own Server
Installation	You don't have to install anything, but just sign up	Install WordPress yourself, either manually or via your host's control panel (if offered)
Themes	Use any theme made available by WordPress.com	Use any theme available anywhere, written by anyone (including yourself)
Plugins	Limited plugin availability	Use any plugin available anywhere, written by anyone (including yourself)

	WordPress.com	**Your Own Server**
Upgrades	WordPress.com provides automatic upgrade	You have to upgrade it yourself when upgrades are available
Widgets	Widget availability depends on available themes	You can widgetize any theme yourself
Maintenance	You don't have to do any maintenance	You're responsible for the maintenance of your site
Advertising	No advertising allowed	Advertise anything and in any amount you like

Building on WordPress.com

WordPress.com (`http://www.wordpress.com`) is a free service provided by the WordPress developers where you can register a blog easily and quickly with no hassle. However, because it is a hosted service, your control over some things will be more limited than it would be if you hosted your own blog. As mentioned before, WordPress.com will not let you edit or upload your own theme. Aside from this, WordPress.com is a great place to maintain your personal blog if you don't need to do anything fancy with a theme.

To register your free blog, click on the loud blue-and-white **Sign Up Now!** button. You will be redirected to the signup page. In the following screenshot, I've entered my username (what I'll sign in with) and a password (note that the password measurement tool will tell you if your password is strong or weak), as well as my email address. Be sure to check the **Legal flotsam** box and leave the **Gimme a blog!** radio button checked. Without it, you won't get a blog.

WORDPRESS.COM

Get your own WordPress.com account in seconds

Fill out this one-step form and you'll be blogging seconds later!

Username	aprilhodgesilver
	(Must be at least 4 characters, letters and numbers only.)
Password	**********
Confirm	**********
	Use upper and lower case characters, numbers and symbols like /"£$%^&/in your password.
	Password Strength:
	Strong
Email Address	april@springthistle.com
	(We send important administration notices to this address so **triple-check** it.)
Legal flotsam	☑ I have read and agree to the fascinating terms of service.
	⦿ Gimme a blog! (Like username.wordpress.com)
	○ Just a username, please.

Next →

After providing this information and clicking on the **Next** button, WordPress will ask for other choices (**Blog Domain**, **Blog Title**, **Language**, and **Privacy**), as shown in following screenshot. You can also check if it's a private blog or not. Note that you cannot change the blog domain later! So be sure it's right.

After providing this information and clicking on **Signup**, you will be sent to a page where you can enter some basic profile information. This page will also tell you that your account is set up, but your email ID needs to be verified. Be sure to check your inbox for the mail with the link and click on it. Then you'll be truly done with the installation.

Now you can skip the next section, which is about installing WordPress manually. You can go directly to the section on the WP Admin panel to start learning about it.

Installing WordPress manually

The WordPress application files can be downloaded for free if you want to do a manual installation. If you've got a website host, this process is extremely easy and requires no previous programming skills or advanced blog user experience. It's a simple ready-set-go blogging engine, where you can easily start even if you are blogging for the first time. Some web hosts even offer automatic installation through the host's online control panel. However, be a little wary of this because some hosts offer automatic installation, but they do it in a way that makes updating your WordPress difficult or awkward.

Preparing the environment

A good first step is to make sure you have an environment set up that is ready for WordPress. This means two things: being sure to verify that the server meets the minimum requirements, and being sure that your database is ready.

As far as web servers go, Apache is the best. But WordPress will also run on a server running the Microsoft server (though you won't be able to use **permalinks**).

Enabling mod_rewrite to use permalinks

If you want to use permalinks, your server must be Unix and Apache's **mod_rewrite** option must be enabled. Apache's mod_rewrite is enabled by default in most web hosting accounts. If you are hosting your own account, you can enable mod_rewrite by modifying the Apache web server configuration file. You can check the URL http://www. tutorio.com/tutorial/enable-mod-rewrite-on-apache to know how to enable mod_rewrite on your web server. If you are running on shared hosting, then ask your system administrator to install it for you. However, it is more likely that you already have it installed on your hosting account.

For WordPress to work, your web host must provide you with a server that does the following two things:

- Support PHP, which must be at least Version 4.3.
- Provide you with write access to a MySQL database. MySQL has to be at least Version 4.0.

You can find out if your host meets these two requirements by contacting your web host. If your web server meets these two basic requirements, you're ready to move on to the next step.

Downloading WordPress

First, you need to download WordPress from `http://wordpress.org/download/`. Take a look at the following screenshot in which the download links are available on the right side:

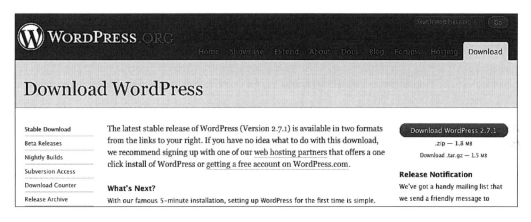

The `.zip` file is shown as a big blue button as most people will need it. If you are using Windows, Mac, or Linux operating systems, your computer will be able to unzip that downloaded file automatically. (The `.tar.gz` file is provided because some Unix users prefer it.)

> **A further note on location**
>
> We're going to cover installing WordPress remotely. However, if you plan to develop themes or plugins, I suggest that you also install a local version. Testing and deploying themes and plugins directly to the remote server will be much more time-consuming than working locally. If you look at the screenshots I'm taking of my own WordPress installation throughout the book, you'll notice that I'm working locally (for example, `http://packt1:8888/` is a local URL).

After you download the WordPress ZIP file, extract the files and you'll get a folder called `wordpress`. This is what it will look like:

Name	Date Modified	Size
index.php	May 25, 2008, 8:33 PM	4 KB
license.txt	Mar 2, 2008, 9:34 PM	1...B
readme.html	Aug 15, 2008, 2:54 AM	8 KB
▷ wp-admin	Oct 23, 2008, 10:50 PM	--
wp-app.php	Jul 22, 2008, 4:04 PM	3...B
wp-atom.php	May 25, 2008, 3:50 PM	4 KB
wp-blog-header.php	May 25, 2008, 3:50 PM	4 KB
wp-comments-post.php	Jun 20, 2008, 8:56 PM	4 KB
wp-commentsrss2.php	May 25, 2008, 3:50 PM	4 KB
wp-config-sample.php	Jul 3, 2008, 5:16 PM	4 KB
▷ wp-content	Oct 23, 2008, 10:50 PM	--
wp-cron.php	May 25, 2008, 3:50 PM	4 KB
wp-feed.php	May 25, 2008, 3:50 PM	4 KB
▷ wp-includes	Oct 23, 2008, 10:50 PM	--
wp-links-opml.php	May 25, 2008, 3:50 PM	4 KB
wp-load.php	Jun 23, 2008, 3:40 PM	4 KB
wp-login.php	Aug 26, 2008, 5:57 PM	2...B
wp-mail.php	May 25, 2008, 3:50 PM	8 KB
wp-pass.php	May 25, 2008, 3:50 PM	4 KB
wp-rdf.php	May 25, 2008, 3:50 PM	4 KB
wp-register.php	May 25, 2008, 3:50 PM	4 KB
wp-rss.php	May 25, 2008, 3:50 PM	4 KB
wp-rss2.php	May 25, 2008, 3:50 PM	4 KB
wp-settings.php	Aug 29, 2008, 6:38 PM	2...B
wp-trackback.php	May 25, 2008, 3:50 PM	4 KB
xmlrpc.php	Jul 24, 2008, 10:08 PM	7...B

Notice that there is a `readme.html` file inside this folder, which gives you a very good introduction to many different features of WordPress.

Uploading the files

Now we need to upload all these files to our web server using any FTP client. There are several FTP clients available on the Internet, which are available either free or as shareware (for a small fee). Take a look at these possibilities if you don't already have an FTP software:

- Filezilla—`http://filezilla-project.org/download.php?type=client` (for Mac or Windows)

- Fetch—`http://fetchsoftworks.com/` (for Mac only)

- SmartFTP—`http://www.smartftp.com/` (for Windows only)

You can also use the popular web-based FTP application net2ftp at `http://www.net2ftp.com`. These services are useful if you don't want to install a desktop application on your computer. You can also check if your host provides browser-based FTP software.

In my screenshots you'll see that I'm using Transmit, which is the professional FTP software I use on my Mac. It works the same way as the examples above.

Using your FTP client or service, connect to your FTP server using the server, username, and password provided to you by your host. Next, open the folder where you want WordPress to live. You may want to install WordPress in your root folder, which will mean that visitors will see your WordPress website's home page when they go to your main URL—for example, `http://yoursite.com`. Or, you may want to install WordPress in a subfolder; for example: `http://yoursite.com/blog/`.

On the left side you will see the files from your local folder, and on the right side you will see your remote folder.

Now select all of the WordPress files on your local machine from the left pane, and drag all of them to the right pane. You can watch as your FTP client uploads the files one at a time and they appear in the right panel.

Once all of the files are done uploading, you're ready to do the installation.

Installing WordPress

Now it's time to install WordPress. For example, I just uploaded all my files to the root of my local website at `http://packt:8888/`. So, this is going to be the URL of my WordPress website. If you access your WordPress URL via your browser, it will look like this:

There doesn't seem to be a `wp-config.php` file. I need this before we can get started. Need more help? We got it. You can create a `wp-config.php` file through a web interface, but this doesn't work for all server setups. The safest way is to manually create the file.

(Create a Configuration File)

It says that you need to create a file named `wp-config.php` before proceeding further. You can click on the **Create a Configuration File** if you want, but it may not work. Your other option, as WordPress recommends, is to do it manually. If you decide to try **Create a Configuration File**, you'll need the information we will soon discuss.

Open the `wordpress` folder and find the file named `wp-config-sample.php`. Make a copy of this file and name it `wp-config.php`. We'll modify this file together. Don't worry; you need not be a PHP programmer. Just open this file with a simple editor such as Notepad. The following is the copied text from the original `wp-config.php` file:

```php
<?php
// ** MySQL settings ** //
define('DB_NAME', 'putyourdbnamehere');    // The name of the database
define('DB_USER', 'usernamehere');      // Your MySQL username
define('DB_PASSWORD', 'yourpasswordhere'); // ...and password
define('DB_HOST', 'localhost');     // 99% chance you won't need to
                                    // change this value
define('DB_CHARSET', 'utf8');
define('DB_COLLATE', '');
```

```
// Change each KEY to a different unique phrase.  You won't have to
remember the phrases later,
// so make them long and complicated.  You can visit http://api.
wordpress.org/secret-key/1.1/
// to get keys generated for you, or just make something up.  Each key
should have a different phrase.
define('AUTH_KEY', 'put your unique phrase here'); // Change this to a
unique phrase.
define('SECURE_AUTH_KEY', 'put your unique phrase here'); // Change
this to a unique phrase.
define('LOGGED_IN_KEY', 'put your unique phrase here'); // Change this
to a unique phrase.

// You can have multiple installations in one database if you give
each a unique prefix
$table_prefix  = 'wp_';    // Only numbers, letters, and underscores
please!

// Change this to localize WordPress.  A corresponding MO file for the
// chosen language must be installed to wp-content/languages.
// For example, install de.mo to wp-content/languages and set WPLANG
to 'de'
// to enable German language support.
define ('WPLANG', '');

/* That's all, stop editing! Happy blogging. */

if ( !defined('ABSPATH') )
    define('ABSPATH', dirname(__FILE__) . '/');
require_once(ABSPATH . 'wp-settings.php');
?>
```

One thing to know about PHP is that any text that comes after a double slash (//), or between a slash-star and star-slash (/*   */), is a comment. It's not actual PHP code. Its purpose is to inform you what that line or that section is about.

As you can see from the previous code, there are a number of settings and parameters that you can set here. However, we'll only worry about the most important ones: the database details.

As I mentioned in an earlier section, you need to have write access to a database. Most large web hosts offer you a way to create your own databases, with usernames and passwords, via an online control panel. If you're not sure how to do this, just email or call your hosting provider for this information. You'll need four pieces of information about your database for the WordPress configuration file. They are:

- Database server—for example, `mysql.yoursite.com`
- Username—for example, `aprilsdbuser`
- Password—for example, `62dcx0hnm`
- Database name—for example, `wptestdb`

Once you have those four things, you can fill them into your `wp-config.php` file. For example, see how mine is filled out here:

```
// ** MySQL settings ** //
define('DB_NAME', 'wptestdb');    // The name of the database
define('DB_USER', 'aprilsdbuser');    // Your MySQL username
define('DB_PASSWORD', '62dcx0hnm'); // ...and password
define('DB_HOST', 'mysql.yoursite.com');    // 99% chance you won't
need to change this value
```

The only other thing you really need to consider is the table prefix. I strongly recommend using a prefix. If you want to install WordPress more than once, you'll need to use different prefixes in your different installations. If you are using this same database for other things, it'll be handy if the tables are grouped based on what they're being used for. So either leave this line as it is, or choose another prefix:

```
// You can have multiple installations in one database if you give
each a unique prefix
$table_prefix  = 'wp_';   // Only numbers, letters, and underscores
please!
```

You may also want to enter three unique phrases for the three keys. This will help to keep your WordPress installation uniquely protected. No one else is likely to choose the same unique keys that you chose, and these will be used when encrypting the passwords for your WordPress users.

Now go back to your browser and re-load the page that's pointing to your WordPress installation. If your configuration file makes sense to WordPress, you'll be taken to the installation page immediately.

Just fill in the name of your blog and your email address, and click on **Install WordPress**. (You can change these later, so don't feel locked into your choices now.) The next page you see will be the last page of the installation!

This page shows you the default **Username**, which is always **admin**, and a randomly generated **Password**.

I suggest you copy that password and paste it into a temporary file on your computer. You'll also need to paste it again in a few minutes when you log in to your WordPress website for the first time.

You can click on **Log In** to get to the login page. Or you can always enter your WordPress Admin panel (also known as the WP Admin) by pointing your browser to http://yoursite.com/wp-admin. If you're not already logged in, this URL will re-direct you to the login page.

If you'd like to see an even more detailed step-by-step guide for manual installation, take a look at this page in the WordPress Codex: http://codex.wordpress.org/ Installing_WordPress.

Learning More

You can find more detailed installation instructions — as well as specifics on changing file permissions, using FTP, using languages, importing from other blogging engines, and more — in the WordPress Codex here: http://codex.wordpress.org/Getting_ Started_with_WordPress#Installation.

Upgrading WordPress from older installations

If you have an older version of WordPress installed, instead of making an entirely new installation, you can upgrade it. Before upgrading, make sure you perform these actions:

- **Back up your database**: You must back up your WordPress database. If anything goes wrong while upgrading, you can lose all of your web site content. Verify that your database backup file is not corrupted. (If your Internet connection breaks during the download, you may have a corrupted file.)

- **Back up your files**: You must back up all your WordPress files in the wordpress folder, even including the .htaccess file. (You'll have one of those if you have been using permalinks.) Verify that none of your files are corrupted by checking a few, especially the last few to download. Make sure that the number of files on your computer and the number of files on your server are the same.

- **Deactivate all your plugins**: Do this via your WP Admin panel. Deactivating plugins is a must, as some plugins may not work with the new version of WordPress you're about to install. As a result, they can cause problems.

 Warning: Do not start the actual upgrade process until you have completed the three steps above. Failing to do so could ruin your upgrade.

The following are the steps to upgrade WordPress:

1. On the server, **delete the following two folders** from your existing WordPress installation:
    - wp-includes
    - wp-admin

2. **Upload the new WordPress files** to your previous WordPress folder except the wp-content folder (see step 6 below). Many, if not all, of the existing files and folders will be overwritten. This is fine for now—you've got a backup, remember?

3. For your `wp-content` folder, you should **copy over the contents, but not the folder itself**. In some cases, copying over the `wp-content` folder itself may delete your customizations and added files.

4. Once the files are uploaded, go to your WP Admin panel and log in, if you're not already logged in. You'll probably be directed to **run an upgrade**. If not, you can go directly to the upgrade page from this URL: `http://yoursite.com/wp-admin/upgrade.php`.

 Now the upgrade itself is complete! The final steps are to restore any site settings that may have been altered during the upgrade.

5. **Re-enable or upgrade your plugins and themes**. Your older plugins and themes may not work with the new version of WordPress. Most developers of popular plugins release new versions of their plugins that are compatible with the newest version of WordPress. You can take a look at the plugin and theme compatibility lists at `http://codex.wordpress.org/Plugins/Plugin_Compatibility` and `http://codex.wordpress.org/Themes/Theme_Compatibility`.

6. **Re-activate** your previously active plugins.

Now you can check over your site and make sure everything is working as you expect. Unless you've upgraded your theme, the frontend of your site should look the same as it did before the upgrade. There's a good chance of the WordPress Admin panel looking different with new features, layout, or colors.

Learning More

If you have any problems with these steps, or if some of them are unclear, you can take a look at the extended WordPress upgrading instructions in the WordPress Codex at `http://codex.wordpress.org/Upgrading_WordPress_Extended`.

The WP Admin panel

WordPress installs a powerful and flexible administration area where you can manage all of your website or blog content, and do much more. Throughout the book, I'll be referring to this in shorthand as the **WP Admin**.

Now that you've successfully installed WordPress, it's time for our first look at the WP Admin. There are some immediate basic changes that I recommend doing right away to make sure your installation is set up properly.

You can always get to the WP Admin by going to this URL: `http://yoursite.com/wp-admin/`. Your first time here, you'll be re-directed to the login page. In the future, WordPress will check to see if you're already logged in and, if so, you'll skip the login page. This is the login page:

To log in, just enter your username, which is by default **admin,** and the password that you got during installation. Then click on **Log In**. Note for the future that on this page there is a link you can use to retrieve your lost password.

Whenever you log in, you'll be taken directly to the **Dashboard** of the WP Admin. Here is a screenshot of the WP Admin that you will see immediately after you log into the blog you just installed:

By default, you are taken to the **Dashboard** just after logging in. You'll see a lot of information and options on the **Dashboard**, which we will explore throughout this book. For now, we will focus on the items that we need to touch upon right after a successful installation. First, let's take a brief look at the top of the WP Admin and the **Dashboard**.

The very top bar, which I'll refer to as the **top menu**, is mostly dark grey and contains:

- A link to your website
- A rollover drop-down menu with oft-handy links to **New Post**, **Drafts**, **New Page**, **Upload**, and **Comments**
- Your username (by default it's **admin**) linked to your profile
- A link to log out
- A link for **Turbo**

You'll also notice the **Screen Options** tab, which appears on many screens within the WP Admin. If you click on it, it will slide down a checklist of items on the page to show or hide. It will be different on each page. I encourage you to play around with that by checking and un-checking items, as you find you need them or don't need them.

On the left, of course, is the **main menu**:

You can click on any word in the main menu to be taken to the main page for that section, or you can click on the rollover arrow to slide down the subpages for that section. For example, if you click on the arrow next to **Settings**, you'll see the subpages for the **Settings** section:

In this book, when describing to you which page within the WP Admin to go to, I'll write things such as "navigate to **Settings | Privacy**" or "navigate to **Posts | Add New**." This always describes a path you can get to via the main menu.

The top menu and the main menu exist on every page within the WP Admin. The main section on the right contains information for the current page you're on. In this case, we're on the **Dashboard**. It contains boxes that have a variety of information about your blog, and about WordPress in general.

For now, we need to do the first thing for a new installation of WordPress: change the password to something easier to remember.

Changing the password

You can change your login information and password from your profile page. To get there, just click on your username in the top menu. Right now, it says **Howdy, admin**.

This will take you to your **Profile** page. You can change a lot of the information on this page. Most notably, you can add your first and last name, change your nickname (this is what will show as the *author* of each post), and add some contact information about yourself. At the very bottom of the page is your opportunity to change your password. You just have to type matching passwords into the **New Password** fields. WordPress has a password **Strength indicator**. It will tell you if your password is easily hackable, based on its length and the presence of mixed-cased letters, numbers, and symbols.

New Password		If you would like to change the password type a new one.
	Otherwise leave this blank.	
		Type your new password again.
	Strength indicator	Hint: Your password should be at least seven characters long. To make it stronger, use upper
and lower case letters, numbers and symbols like ! " ? $ % ^ &).		

Once you've added or changed everything you want to on this page, click on the **Update Profile** button at the bottom of the page. Your information will be saved and you'll see a message at the top of the page telling you that the save was successful.

Changing general blog information

You may need to change and add some general blog information (such as blog title, one-sentence description, and so on) after a successful installation to kick-start blogging. To get started with general blog information, navigate to **Settings** in the main menu.

There are many options you can set here, most of which are pretty self-explanatory. We'll look at the most important ones and you can explore the rest on your own. Obviously, you can change your blog's title. You can see from my screenshots that I've called mine **April's Food Blog**:

General Settings		Help
Blog Title	April's Food Blog	
Tagline	Just another WordPress weblog	In
	a few words, explain what this blog is about.	

You can also change the blog description, which is used in most themes as a subtitle for the blog, like the subtitle of a book. The default description is **Just another WordPress weblog**. You'll probably want to change that!

The next important thing to consider is the **Membership** box:

Membership	Anyone can register
New User Default Role	Subscriber

By default, none of your visitors can register for your blog. If you want visitors to be able to create an account on your blog, you have to check this box. Once people register, you can choose to elevate them from **Subscriber**, which is their default role, to a role with more power.

The box below, which is labeled **New User Default Role**, should stay at **Subscriber**. If you change it to anything else, complete strangers will be able to create an account on your blog and start posting. This can be quite risky, as you never know what complete strangers will say.

The only other thing you may want to change is the time and date settings of your blog—if they are not automatically correct. When you're done making changes to this page, be sure to click on the **Save Changes** button at the bottom of the page.

Your first post

Now it's time to starting blogging. The core of any blog is the blog posts, so you are going to make your first post. (This won't be the very first post on the blog itself, because WordPress created a post, a comment, and a page for you when it installed. It will be YOUR first post, however!). To create a post, just click on **New Post** on the top menu. You'll be taken to this page:

As you can see, there are a lot of options for your post (which we'll explore in more detail in Chapter 3). For now, just worry about the basics. Every post should have, at minimum, a title and some content. So go ahead and write in some text for those two things. When you are happy with it, click on the **Publish** button.

You'll get a yellow note telling you that the post is published. Take a look at the front page of your site by clicking on **Visit site** in the top menu, next to your blog's name. You'll see this:

Your first comment

Now let's see what it's like to post a comment. One of the great things about blogs is that they give you, the writer, the opportunity to spark a conversation with your readers. WordPress comes with a fantastic commenting system that allows visitors to add comments to your blog. To add your own comment to your first post, click on the **No Comments** link underneath your first post. You'll be taken to the post's individual page at the bottom, where you can find a comment form like this:

Leave a Reply

Logged in as admin. Log out »

Submit Comment

Your visitors, who won't already be logged into the WP Admin, will see a form that looks like this instead:

Leave a Reply

Name (required)

Mail (will not be published) (required)

Website

Submit Comment

Since you're already logged in, all you have to do is write something in the text area and click on **Submit Comment**. Then you'll see your comment show up under the post, and that's it. Later, we'll explore how you can control which comments show up right away and which comments have to wait for you to verify them as valid.

Retrieving a lost password

If you have lost your password and can't get into your WP Admin panel, you can easily retrieve your password by clicking on the **Lost your password?** link on the login page. A newly generated password will be emailed to you at the email address you gave during the WordPress installation. This is why you need to be sure to enter a valid email address. Otherwise, you will not be able to retrieve your password.

Summary

You have learned a lot of things from this chapter. Now you are able to install WordPress on a remote server, change the basic default settings of your blog, write posts, and comment on those posts.

In the next chapter we will learn how to make a blog post and how to control all of the information for that post. In the meantime, feel free to experiment with the things you learned to do in this chapter to become more comfortable with them.

3
Blogging Your Heart Out

Now that your WordPress installation is up and running, you are ready to start blogging. You've made the right choice with WordPress because it's quite a powerful tool with a seemingly infinite array of options and possibilities.

In this chapter, you will learn how to make a blog post and how to control all of the information for that post, and not just the title and content. You will also learn about comments—what they are for and how to manage them. Additionally, we will explore how to keep your content organized and searchable using tags and categories.

Posting on your blog

The central activity you'll be doing with your blog is adding posts. A **post** is like an article in a magazine; it's got a title, content, and an author (you). If a blog is like an online diary, then every post is an entry in that diary. A blog post also has a lot of other information attached to it, such as a date and categories. In this section, you will learn how to create a new post and what kind of information you can attach to it.

Adding a simple post

Let's review the process of adding a simple post to your blog, which we carried out in the previous chapter. Whenever you want to do maintenance on your WordPress website, you have to start by logging in to the **WP Admin (WordPress Administration panel)** for your site. To get to the admin panel, just point your web browser to `http://yoursite.com/wp-admin`.

Remember that if you have installed WordPress in a subfolder (for example, `blog`), then your URL has to include the subfolder (that is, `http://yoursite.com/blog/wp-admin`).

When you first log in to the WP Admin, you'll be at the **Dashboard**. The **Dashboard** has a lot of information on it; but don't worry about that right now. We'll discuss the **Dashboard** in detail later in the book.

The quickest way to get to the **Add New Post** page at any time is to click on the **New Post** link at the top of the page in the top bar (top menu).

This is the **Add New Post** page:

To quickly add a new post to your site, all you have to do is:

1. Type in a title into the text field under **Add New Post** (for example, **Making Lasagne**).

2. Type the text of your post in the content box. Note that the default view is **Visual**, but you actually have a choice of the **HTML** view as well.

3. Click on the **Publish** button, which is at the far right. Note that you can choose to save a draft or view a preview of your post.

In the following image, the title field, the content box, and the **Publish** button of the **Add New Post** page are highlighted:

Once you click on the **Publish** button, you have to wait while WordPress performs its magic. You'll see yourself still on the **Edit Post** page, but now the following message has appeared telling you that your post was published and giving you a link to **View post**:

If you go to the front page of your site, you'll see that your new post has been added at the top (newest posts are always at the top):

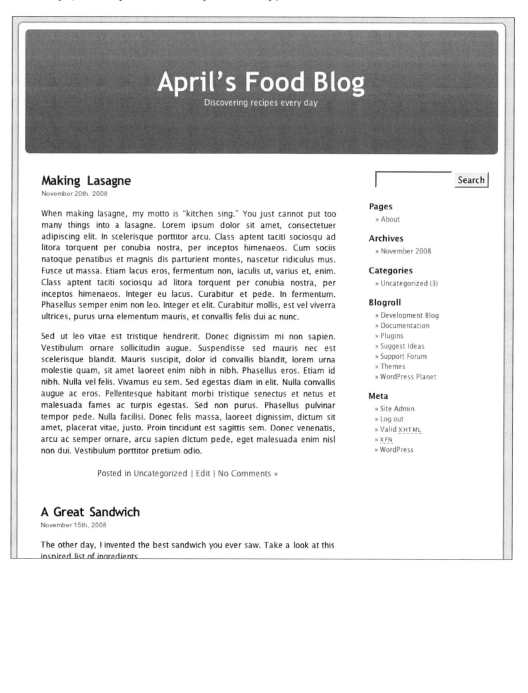

Common post options

Now that we've reviewed the basics of adding a post, let's investigate some of the other options on the **Add New Post** page. In this section we'll look at the most commonly used options, and in the next section we'll look at the more advanced options.

Categories and tags

Categories and tags are two similar types of information that you can add to a blog post. We use them to organize the information in your blog by topic and content (rather than just by, say, date), and to help visitors find what they are looking for on your blog.

Categories are primarily used for structural organizing. They can be hierarchical. A relatively busy blog will probably have at least 10 categories, but probably not more than 15 or 20. Each post in this blog will likely have one to four categories assigned to it. For example, a blog about food might have these categories: **Cooking Adventures**, **In The Media**, **Ingredients**, **Opinion**, **Recipes Found**, **Recipes Invented**, and **Restaurants**.

Tags are primarily used as shorthand for describing the topics covered in a particular blog post. A relatively busy blog will have anywhere from 15 to 30 tags in use. Each post in this blog will likely have three to ten tags assigned to it. For example, a post on the food blog about a recipe for butternut squash soup may have these tags: **soup, vegetarian, autumn, hot, easy**.

Let's add a new post to the blog. This time, we'll give it not only a title and content, but also tags and categories. When adding tags, just type your list of tags into the **Tags** box on the right, separated by commas:

Tags
soup, vegetarian, autumn,   (Add)
Separate tags with commas
Choose from the most popular tags

Then click on the **Add** button. The tags you just typed in will appear below the text field with little **x**s next to them. You can click on an **x** to delete a tag. Once you've used some tags in your blog, you'll be able to click on the **Choose from the most popular tags** link in this box so that you can easily re-use tags.

Categories work a bit differently than tags. Once you get your blog going, you'll usually just check the boxes next to existing categories in the **Categories** box. In this case, as we don't have any existing categories, we'll have to add one or two.

In the **Categories** box on the right, click on the **+ Add New Category** link. Type your category into the text field and click on the **Add** button. Your new category will show up in the list, already checked. Look at the following screenshot:

If in the future you want to add a category that needs a parent category, select **Parent category** from the pull-down menu before clicking on the **Add** button. If you want to manage more details about your categories, move them around, rename them, assign parent categories, and assign descriptive text. You can do this on the **Categories** page, which we'll see in detail later in this chapter.

Now fill in your title and content here:

Click on the **Publish** button and you're done. When you look at the front page of your site, you'll see your new post on the top, your new category in the sidebar, and the tags and category (that you chose for your post) listed under the post itself:

Adding an image to a post

You may often want to have an image show up in your post. WordPress makes this very easy. Let's add an image to the post we just created. You can click on **Edit** underneath your post on the front page of your site to get there quickly. Alternatively, go back to the WP Admin, open **Posts** in the main menu, and then click on **Edit** underneath your new post.

To add an image to a post, first you'll need to have that image on your computer. Before you get ready to upload an image, make sure that your image is optimized for the Web. Huge files will be uploaded slowly and slow down the process of viewing your site. You can re-size and optimize images using software such as GIMP or Photoshop. For the example in this chapter, I have used a photo of butternut squash soup that I have taken from the website where I got the recipe, and I know it's on the desktop of my computer. Once you have a picture on your computer and know where it is, follow these steps to add the photo to your blog post:

1. Click on the little photo icon, which is next to the word **Upload/Insert** and below the box for the title:

2. In the box that appears, click on the **Select Files** button and browse to your image. Then click on **Open** and watch the uploader bar. When it's done, you'll have a number of fields you can fill in:

The only fields that are important right now are **Title**, **Alignment**, and **Size**. **Title** is a description for the image, **Alignment** will tell the image whether to have text wrap around it, and **Size** is the size of the image. As you can see, I've chosen the **Right** alignment and the **Thumbnail** size.

3. Now click on **Insert into Post**. This box will disappear, and your image will show up in the post on the edit page itself:

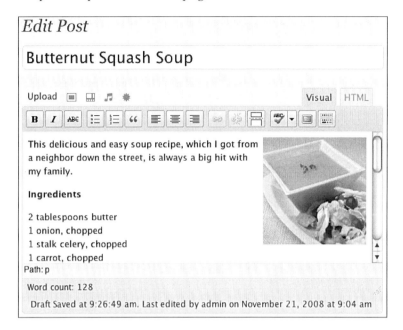

4. Now click on the **Update Post** button and go look at the front page of your site again. There's your image!

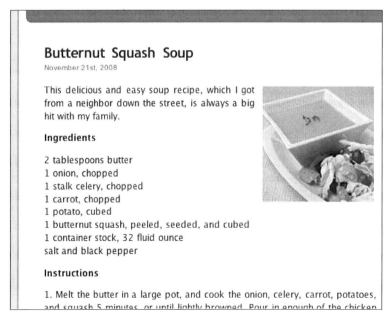

You may be wondering about those image sizes. What if you want bigger or smaller thumbnails? You can set the pixel dimensions of your uploaded images and other preferences by opening **Settings** in the main menu and then clicking on **Media**. This takes you to the **Media Settings** page:

Here you can specify the size of the uploaded images for:

- **Thumbnail**
- **Medium**
- **Large**

If you change the dimensions on this page and click on the **Save Changes** button, only images you upload in the future will be affected. Images you've already uploaded to the site will have had their thumbnail, medium, and large versions created already using the old dimensions.

Using the Visual editor versus the HTML editor

WordPress comes with a Visual editor, otherwise known as a **WYSIWYG** editor (pronounced wissy-wig, which stands for **What You See Is What You Get**). This is the default editor for typing and editing your posts. If you're comfortable with HTML, you may prefer to write and edit your posts using the HTML editor—particularly useful if you want to add special content or styling.

To switch from the rich text editor to the HTML editor, click on the **HTML** tab next to the **Visual** tab at the top of the content box:

You'll see your post in all its raw HTML glory and you'll get a new set of buttons that lets you quickly bold and italicize text as well as add link code, image code, and so on.

You can make changes and swap back and forth between the tabs to see the result.

 If you want the **HTML** tab to be your default editor, you can change this on your **Profile** page. Navigate to **Users | Your Profile**, and select the **Disable the visual editor when writing** checkbox.

Drafts, timestamps, and managing posts

There are three additional, simple but common, items I'd like to cover in this section: drafts, timestamps, and managing posts.

Drafts

WordPress gives you the option to save a draft of your post so that you don't have to publish it right away but can still save your work. If you've started writing a post and want to save a draft, just click on the **Save Draft** button at the right (in the **Publish** box), instead of the **Publish** button. Even if you don't click on the **Save Draft** button, WordPress will attempt to save a draft of your post for you about once a minute. You'll see this in the area just below the content box. The text will say **Saving Draft...** and then the time of the last draft saved:

Start with good mushrooms. That's the most important part.

Path: p

Word count: 1   Draft Saved at 9:40:56 am.

At this point, after a manual save or an auto-save, you can leave the **Edit Post** page and do other things. You'll be able to access all of your draft posts from the **Dashboard** or from the **Edit Posts** page.

Timestamps

WordPress will also let you alter the timestamp of your post. This is useful if you are writing a post today that you wish you'd published yesterday, or if you're writing a post in advance and don't want it to show up until the right day. The default timestamp will always be set to the moment you publish your post. To change it, just find the **Publish** box and click on the **Edit** link (next to the calendar icon and **Publish immediately**), and fields will show up with the current date and time for you to change:

Change the details, click on the **OK** button, and then **Publish** your post (or save a draft).

Managing posts

If you want to see a list of your posts so that you can easily skim and manage them, you just need to go to the **Edit Posts** page in the WP Admin by navigating to **Posts** in the main menu. You'll see a detailed list of your posts, as seen in the next screenshot:

Post	Author	Categories	Tags	💬	Date
Creamy Mushroom Pasta – **Draft**	admin	Uncategorized	No Tags	0	2008/11/21 Last Modified
Butternut Squash Soup Edit | Quick Edit | Delete | View	admin	Recipes Found	autumn, easy, hot, soup, vegetarian	0	48 mins ago Published
Making Lasagne	admin	Uncategorized	No Tags	0	22 hours ago Published
A Great Sandwich	admin	Uncategorized	No Tags	0	2008/11/15 Published
Hello world!	admin	Uncategorized	No Tags	1	2008/11/12 Published
Post	Author	Categories	Tags	💬	Date

Edit Posts

All (5) | Published (4) | Draft (1)

Bulk Actions | Apply   Show all dates | View all categories | Filter

Screen Options ▾   Help ▾

Search Posts

Bulk Actions | Apply

There are so many things you can do on this page! You can:

- Choose a post to edit—click on a post title and you'll go back to the main **Edit Post** page
- Quick-edit a post—click on the **Quick Edit** link for any post and new options will appear right in the list, which will let you edit the title, timestamp, categories, tags, and more
- Delete one or more posts—click on the checkboxes next to the posts you want to delete, choose **Delete** from the **Bulk Actions** drop-down menu at the bottom, and click on the **Apply** button
- Bulk edit posts—choose **Edit** from the **Bulk Actions** menu at the bottom, click on the **Apply** button, and you'll be able to assign categories and tags to multiple posts, as well as edit other information about them

You can experiment with the other links and options on this page. Just click on the pull-down menus and links, and see what happens.

Advanced post options

By now, you have a handle on the most common and simple options for posts and you may be wondering about some of the other options on the **Edit Post** page. We'll cover them all in this section.

A quick display tip:

When you first visit the **Edit Post** page, all of the four advanced options (**Excerpt**, **Send Trackbacks**, **Custom Fields**, and **Discussion**) are 'open' below the post content. If you never use them and want to clean up the look of this page, you can single-click each bar and they'll collapse. You can also rearrange them by dragging them to a new order.

You can also use **Screen Options** (top right of the page) to uncheck certain boxes, and thus not display them at all.

Excerpt

WordPress offers theme designers the option to show a post's excerpt (instead of its full content) on pages within the theme. If you enter some text into the excerpt box on the **Edit Post** page, that text will be used as the post's excerpt on theme pages that call for it. However, if there is no text in this box, WordPress will use the first 55 words of the post's content (which is stripped of HTML tags) followed by **[...]** (which is not a link).

The `<!-- more -->` tag should not be confused with the excerpt. This is different from the excerpt because you, not the theme designer control its use. Text before this tag, for any post that has it, will be the only thing that's shown on all blog pages (for example homepage, category page, search results page, and so on). The full post text will only show up on the post page. All you have to do is put the `<!-- more -->` link at the spot in your post where you'd like the cut-off to be. WordPress will automatically cut off the post there and replace it with a **Read the rest of this post** link.

To add this tag to a post, first place your cursor in the spot where you'd like the post to be split up. Then click on the **more** tag button in the editor. If you're using the Visual editor, the button you want to click looks like this:

If you're using the HTML editor, the button looks like this:

Trackbacks

Trackbacks are useful if you write a blog post that is a response to a post on someone else's blog and you want them to know about it. Just copy the trackback URL from that person's blog post and paste it into this box. An excerpt of your blog post will show up as a comment on their blog post.

If someone wants to display a blog post on their blog about a post on your blog using the default theme, he or she can find the trackback URL on the post page for every post. For example, click on the title of one of your posts on your blogs' front page and you'll go to the post page:

A Great Sandwich

The other day, I invented the best sandwich you ever saw. Take a look at this inspired list of ingredients.

Aliquam sagittis euismod quam. Mauris et justo. Etiam ipsum arcu, ullamcorper sit amet, laoreet ac, dignissim dapibus, ligula. Pellentesque habitant morbi tristique senectus et netus et malesuada fames ac turpis egestas. Cras dictum, lectus in faucibus suscipit, pede lacus egestas elit, eget sagittis nulla metus at augue. Curabitur risus. Duis ligula urna, malesuada non, congue sed, lobortis sed, lectus. Nulla facilisi. Pellentesque elementum semper risus. Nam id dui. Quisque euismod elit ac ligula. Nulla blandit. Suspendisse potenti. Vestibulum leo purus, sollicitudin non, tempor at, scelerisque vitae, leo.

This entry was posted on Saturday, November 15th, 2008 at 11:39 am and is filed under Uncategorized . You can follow any responses to this entry through the RSS 2.0 feed. You can leave a response, or trackback from your own site. Edit this entry.

All this person has to do is right-click on the **trackback** link and select **Copy Link Location**, which in this case is `http://packt:8888/2008/11/a-great-sandwich/trackback/`. If permalinks are not turned on, it would be `http://packt:8888/wp-trackback.php?p=6`.

Trackbacks are becoming somewhat out-of-date with the advent of pinging. In fact, many WordPress themes are written to essentially disable trackbacks. **Pinging** is WordPress's way of notifying popular update services, such as Ping-o-Matic!, which other people use to keep up-to-date with your blog and other people's blogs. We will explain more about pinging in the following section.

Discussion

A **Discussion** box has two checkboxes in it: one for allowing comments, and the other for trackbacks and pingbacks. When you first install WordPress, both these checkboxes will be checked by default. You have to uncheck them if you want to turn off the comments or trackbacks and pingbacks for the post.

Pingbacks are essentially the same as trackbacks, but differ in two important ways:

- The notification from your blog to the blog of the person you're commenting on happens automatically—you don't have to enter a special URL into a special field. All you have to do is link your blog post to their blog post.

- Pingbacks don't send any content.

If you uncheck the **comments** box, visitors will not be able to comment on this blog post.

If you uncheck the **trackbacks and pingbacks** box, when other people mention your blog post and link to it on their own websites, your blog post won't notice and won't care. So, if you are using WordPress to run a non-blog website, this is the best option for you.

If the box stays checked, other people's pingbacks about this post will show up under your post along with comments, if any. If you're using WordPress to run a blog website, you'll want pingback to stay checked—especially if you want sites such as Technorati and other rating/authority sites to stay alerted.

If you want either or both of these boxes to be unchecked by default, go to **Settings** and then **Discussion** in the main menu. You can uncheck either or both of the boxes labeled **Allow link notifications from other blogs (pingbacks and trackbacks.)** and **Allow people to post comments on the article**:

Discussion Settings

Default article settings

☐ Attempt to notify any blogs linked to from the article (slows down posting.)

☑ Allow link notifications from other blogs (pingbacks and trackbacks.)

☑ Allow people to post comments on the article

(These settings may be overridden for individual articles.)

Learning more:

To learn more about trackbacks and pingbacks you can visit the following sites:

- `http://www.tamba2.org.uk/wordpress/ping/`
- `http://codex.wordpress.org/Introduction_to_Blogging#Trackbacks`
- `http://codex.wordpress.org/Introduction_to_Blogging#Pingbacks`

Custom Fields

Custom Fields are a way for you to add additional information about your blog posts that are not part of WordPress by default. By default, every WordPress post has a number of pieces of information (fields) such as title, content, date, categories, and so on. If there is a field you want all or many of your posts to have, you can add it here.

For example, let's say you are a gadget reviewer and every blog post is a review of some new gadget. Every time you write a review, you're writing it about a product made by some company, and you'd like to have that company's logo associated with the blog post. You can make a custom field called **company_logo** and the value can be the path to the logo image.

To use this custom field information, you either have to manually modify your theme files, or use a plugin.

Learning more

Read more about custom fields in the WordPress codex at
`http://codex.wordpress.org/Using_Custom_Fields`.

Password and private protection

WordPress gives you the option to hide posts. You can hide a post from everyone but yourself by marking it **Private**, or you can hide it from everyone but the people with whom you share a password by marking it as **Password protected**. To implement this, look at the **Publish** box at the upper right of the **Edit Post** page. If you click on the **Edit** link next to **Visibility: Public**, a few options will appear:

> Visibility: **Public**
> ⊙ Public
> ☐ Stick this post to the front page
> ○ Password protected
> ○ Private
>
> (OK) Cancel

If you click on the **Password protected** radio button, you'll get a box where you can type a password. Visitors to your blog will see the post title along with a note that they have to type in a password to read the post.

If you click on the **Private** radio button, the post will not show up on the blog at all to any viewers, unless you are the viewer and you are logged in.

If you leave the post **Public** and check the **Stick this post to the front page** checkbox, this post will be the first post on the front page, regardless of its publication date.

Be sure to click on the **OK** button if you make any changes.

Post slug

This box may not be visible by default, in which case you have to open **Screen Options** at the top of the page and check the box next to **Post Slug**.

The post slug is used in the URL if your blog is using permalinks. **Permalinks** are a way to prettify your URLs. For example, right now, the URL for my **Butternut Squash soup** post is `http://packt:8888/?p=10`. If I turn on permalinks, by default the URL would be `http://packt:8888/2008/11/butternut-squash-soup/`. The very last part of the URL, `butternut-squash-soup`, is the slug. WordPress chose the slug by taking my post title, making it all lowercase, removing all punctuation, and replacing spaces with dashes. If I'd prefer it to be something else, such as `squash-soup`, this **Post Slug** box is where I can change it. The slug is something that Google search loves, so using them helps to optimize your site for search engines.

Additional writing options

Aside from simply logging into the WP Admin, you have two other choices for adding posts to your blog.

Press This

WordPress offers a neat bookmark called **Press This**. You can put it into your browser's bookmarks or favorites, which will let you quickly write a blog post about the website you're visiting. (This used to be called the **bookmarklet**.) You may have encountered this same feature as offered by Facebook, Del.ico.us, and other social networking sites.

You just have to add **Press This** to your browser once, and then you can use it anytime. To add the **Press This** link to your browser in the WP Admin, go to the **Tools** menu. At the bottom of the **Tools** page is a **Press This** link. Just grab it with your mouse and drag it up to your browser's bookmark bar.

Now it's available to you. For example, if you're reading a newspaper website and you read an article you'd like to mention in a blog post, just click the **Press This** bookmark (or favorite). A window will pop up with the **Edit Post** page in it and the URL of the site you're looking at already written in as a link:

You can then write whatever additional text you want, add tags and categories, and then either save it as a draft or publish it right away.

Posting via email

If you want to add a post to your blog without having to open the WP Admin and log in, you can set up your WordPress installation to accept posts sent via email. First, you have to set up a special secret email address that is accessible via POP. WordPress will check that email address and turn any emails in it into posts. So you have to be sure not to use this email address for any other purpose!

Once you have the email address set up at your mail server, go to your WP Admin and navigate to **Settings | Writing**. Scroll down a bit to **Post via e-mail**:

Now just enter the server, login name, and password into the **Writing Settings** page and be sure to click on the **Save Changes** button.

Discussion on your blog—comments

Comments are an important part of most of the blogs. While you are the only person who can write blog posts, the visitors to your blog can add comments to your posts. This can fuel a sense of community within a blog, allow people to give you feedback on your writing, and give your visitors a way to help or talk to other visitors. The only downside of commenting is that unscrupulous people will try to misuse your blog's ability to accept comments, and will try to post spam or advertisements in your blog instead of relevant comments. Luckily, the WordPress community is always developing more ways of fighting spam.

Adding a comment

If you look at the front page of your blog, you'll see that every post has a link that says **No Comments** » at the bottom. Clicking on that link will take you to the bottom of the post page, which is where comments can be added:

If you're logged into the WP Admin, you'll see your name and a space where to write your comment. If you're not logged in, you'll see a comment form that any other visitor will see. This form includes fields to fill in for name, email, and website, along with the commenting text area.

Once you type in the required information and click on the **Submit Comment** button, the comment will get entered into the WordPress database along with all of your other blog information. How soon it shows up on the site depends on your discussion settings.

Discussion settings

In the screenshot above, notice that **Name** and **Mail** are both marked as **(required)**. As the owner of this blog, you can change the requirements for post comments. First, log in to the WP Admin and navigate to **Settings | Discussion**. We explored the first box (**Default article settings**) earlier in this chapter.

Submission, notification, and moderation settings

Let's take a look at the next three boxes:

Other comment settings	☑ Comment author must fill out name and e-mail
	☐ Users must be registered and logged in to comment
	☐ Automatically close comments on articles older than 14 days
	☐ Enable threaded (nested) comments 5 ▾ levels deep
	☑ Break comments into pages with 50 comments per page and the last ▾ page displayed by default
	Comments should be displayed with the older ▾ comments at the top of each page
E-mail me whenever	☑ Anyone posts a comment
	☑ A comment is held for moderation
Before a comment appears	☐ An administrator must always approve the comment
	☑ Comment author must have a previously approved comment

The boxes you check in these sections will determine how much moderation and checking a comment has to go through before it gets posted on the blog. In the screenshot we just saw, the settings shown are the default settings, which are pretty strict. The only way to make a more strictly controlled discussion on your blog is to check **An administrator must always approve the comment**. This option means that no matter what, all comments go into the moderation queue and do not show up on the site till you manually approve them.

Let's look at the settings having to do with *submission*. These two options, which are in the **Other comment settings** box, control what the user has to do before he or she is even able to type in a comment:

- **Comment author must fill out name and e-mail**

  As you noticed in the screenshot in the *Adding a comment* section, **Name** and **Mail** are marked **(required)**. If you leave this checked, then anyone posting a comment will encounter an error if they try to leave either of the fields blank. This doesn't add a huge amount of security because robots know how to fill out a name and an email, and because anyone can put fake information in there. However, it does help your blog readers to keep a track of who is who if a long discussion develops, and it can slightly discourage the utterly impulsive commenting.

- **Users must be registered and logged in to comment**

  Most bloggers do not check this box because it means that only visitors who register for the blog can comment. Most bloggers don't want random people registering, and most visitors don't want to be compelled to register for your blog. If you check this box, there's a good chance you'll get no comments (which may be what you want). Or, if you're setting up a blog for a closed community of people, this setting might be useful.

Now let's look at the settings that have to do with *moderation*. These two options, which have to do with the circumstances that allow comments to appear on the site, are in the **Before a comment appears** box:

- **An administrator must always approve the comment**

  As I mentioned before, if this box is checked, every comment has to be manually approved by you before it appears on the site.

- **Comment author must have a previously approved comment**

  If you uncheck the box above this, but check this one, then you've relaxed your settings a little bit. This means that if the person commenting has commented before and had his or her comment approved, then the person's future comments don't have to be verified by you; they'll just appear on the website immediately. The person just has to enter the same name and email as the previously approved comment.

Now let's look at the settings that have to do with *notification*. These two options are in the **Email me whenever** box. These options are related to the circumstances of receiving an email notification about the comment activity.

- **Anyone posts a comment**

  This is generally a good setting to keep. You'll get an email whenever anyone posts a comment—whether or not it needs to be moderated. This will make it easier for you to follow the discussion on your blog, and to be quickly aware of a comment that is not moderated and requires deletion.

- **A comment is held for moderation**

  If you're not particularly interested in following every comment on your blog, you can uncheck the **Anyone posts a comment** checkbox and only leave this one checked. You won't get an email about legitimate-looking comments that don't appear to need moderation, but only those that need your approval.

The remaining settings, which are all in the **Other comment settings** box, have to do with *comment display* and are pretty self-explanatory. You won't be able to see many of these settings in action until you have lots of comments.

When to moderate or blacklist a comment

If you scroll down the page a bit, you'll see the **Comment Moderation** box:

This an extension of the moderation settings from the top of the page. Note that if you've checked the **An administraor must approve the comment** checkbox, you can safely ignore this **Comment Moderation** box. Otherwise, you can use this box to help WordPress figure out which comments are probably OK and which might be spam or inappropriate for your blog. You can tell WordPress to suspect a comment if it has more than a certain number of links, as spam comments often are just a list of URLs.

The larger box is for you to enter suspect words and IP addresses:

- Here you can type words that are commonly found in spam (you can figure this out by looking in your junk mail in your email!), or just uncouth words in general.

- The IP addresses you will enter into this box would be those of any comments you've gotten in the past from someone who comments inappropriately or adds actual spam. Whenever WordPress receives a comment on your blog, it captures the IP address for you so that you'll have them handy.

Scroll down a bit more and you'll see the **Comment Blacklist** box:

Unlike the **Comment Moderation** box we just saw, which tells WordPress how to identify the comments to suspect, the **Comment Blacklist** box tells WordPress how to identify comments that are almost definitely bad. These comments won't be added to the moderation queue and you won't get an email about them; they'll be marked right away as spam.

Avatar display settings

The final box on this page is the **Avatars** box:

An **avatar** is an image that is a person's personal icon. Visitors who are very active on the Internet and comment frequently may have set up an avatar that they like to use. If so, it will show up on your blog if you leave the **Show Avatars** radio button checked.

The second box, **Maximum Rating**, will tell WordPress if it should not show avatars that have been rated too highly.

The third box, **Default Avatar**, tells WordPress what avatar to use for visitors who do not come with their own avatar. When you installed WordPress, it created a comment for you on the first post, and also created a default avatar for you. You can see the default avatar, **Mystery Man**, at use on the **Hello World!** post:

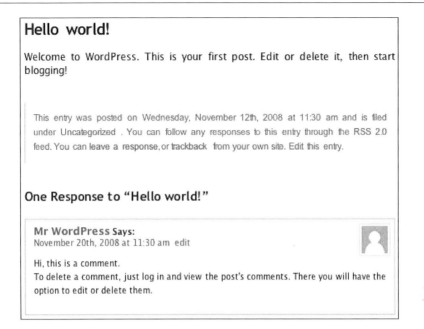

Moderating comments

Now that we've thoroughly explored the settings for which comments need to be moderated, let's discuss what you actually need to do to moderate comments. Moderating means that you look over a comment that is in limbo and decide whether it's good or bad. If it's good, it gets to appear on the website; and if it is bad, it's either marked as spam or is deleted and is never seen by anyone but you and the poster who wrote it.

To view comments waiting for moderation, log in to your WP Admin and navigate to **Comments** in the main menu.

If you have any comments waiting for moderation, there will be a little orange number in the main menu telling you how many comments await moderation.

This **Edit Comments** page is fully featured, just like the **Edit Posts** page. For each comment, you see the following information from left to right:

- Comment text, along with links to **Approve** it so that it shows up on the site, mark it as **Spam**, **Delete** it, **Edit** it, **Quick Edit** it, or **Reply** to it

- Commenter name, avatar, email address, and IP

- Comment submission time and date

- The title of the post on which the comment was made (which is also a link to edit that post), a number in parentheses indicating how many approved comments are already there on that post (which is also a link that will filter the comments list so that it shows only comments on this page), and a link to the post itself (indicated with a hash **#**)

Comments that are awaiting moderation have a yellow background.

You can click on the **Quick Edit** link for any post to open form fields right within this list. This will allow you to edit the text of the post and the commenter's name, email, and URL.

You can use the links at the top—**All**, **Pending**, **Approved**, and **Spam**—to filter the list based on those statuses. You can also filter either only pings or comments with the **Show all comment types** pull-down filter menu. You can check one or more comments to apply any of the bulk actions available in the **Bulk Actions** menus at the top and bottom of the list.

Another quick way to get to this page, or to apply an action to a comment, is to use the links in the email WordPress sends you when a comment is held for moderation.

How to eliminate comment spam

Comment spam are comments that get posted on your blog that have spam content, just like spam email. If you've set up your moderation settings to be relatively secure, then these comments won't appear on your blog. However, you may get dozens of email a day from WordPress asking you to moderate comments that it knows need moderation, but doesn't know are spam.

The best tool available for eliminating comment spam from your blog is the Akismet plugin. This plugin, which comes (though inactive) with your WordPress installation, utilizes the Akismet spam-fighting service. We'll be discussing plugins in more detail later in this book. For now, we'll review how to get Akismet working on your blog. If your blog is built on WordPress.com, then Akismet is already activated by default on your blog.

Learning more

You can learn more about the Akismet spam-fighting service from `http://akismet.com/`.

Getting a WordPress.com API key

The Akismet plugin requires that you have a WordPress.com API key. To get one, you have to create an account at WordPress.com, even if you don't have a blog there. Follow the instructions in Chapter 2 to create an account at WordPress.com. Once your account is active, log in to WordPress.com and use the menu at the very top to go to your profile:

When you are on the **Your Profile** page, you'll see your **WordPress.com API key** right at the top:

Select and copy that text. You may want to paste it into a text file to be sure you have it.

Activating Akismet

Now go back to your WordPress installation and navigate to **Plugins** in the main menu:

You'll see Akismet listed as the first plugin. Click on the **Activate** link. A yellow message bar will appear at the top of the page that says **Akismet is almost ready. You must enter your WordPress.com API key for it to work.** Click on that link and you'll be taken to a page where you can enter your API key you have copied from WordPress.com:

Paste your API key into the box. I suggest you also check the box below it about automatically discarding spam comments. Akismet is very good at identifying which comments are actually spam, and checking this box will make them disappear. However, if you're concerned about Akismet misidentifying comments, leave this unchecked.

Now click on **Update options>>** and your blog is protected from comment spam!

Adding and managing categories

Earlier in this chapter, you learned how to quickly add a category when adding a post. Now let's talk about how to manage your categories in a bigger way. First, navigate to **Posts | Categories** in your WP Admin. You'll see the **Categories** page:

This is a useful page that combines the ability to add, edit, and review all of your categories. As you can see, any categories you've added via the **Edit Post** page are listed. You can **Edit**, **Quick Edit**, or **Delete** any category by clicking on the appropriate link in the list.

If you add a category on this page, you can also choose its slug. The **slug** is the short bit of text that shows up in the URL of your site if you have permalinks enabled. If you don't choose a slug, WordPress will create one for you by taking the category name, reducing it to all lowercase, replacing spaces with dashes, and removing any other punctuation marks.

Another thing you can do on this page is choose a parent category for any category. If you choose to use parent categories, your categories will be displayed hierarchically, just as your pages are displayed.

Summary

In this chapter, you learned everything you need to know to add content to your blog and manage that content. You learned about posts, categories, and comments. You discovered tags, spam, and excerpts. You also learned about adding images, using the rich text editor, changing timestamps, customizing excerpts, and the different ways of posting.

Your control of your blog content is complete and you are well equipped to set your blog on fire!

In the next chapter, you'll learn about all the other types of content that you can manage on your website with WordPress.

4
Pages, Images, Plugins, and More

You now have the blog part of your website fully under control. By now you may have noticed that WordPress offers you a lot more than simply posts, comments, and categories.

In this chapter, we will explore and control all of the other content types that WordPress already has. You'll be able to create static pages that aren't a part of your ongoing blog, bookmark links that will drive visitors to your friends, and add and manage built-in image galleries to display photos and other images. You'll also learn how to add plugins, which will enhance the capabilities of your entire website.

Pages

At first glance, pages look very similar to posts. They also have a title and a content area in which we can write extended text. However, pages are handled quite differently from posts. Pages don't have a timestamp, categories, or tags. Posts belong to your blog, which is meant to be a part of an ongoing expanding section of your website, and are added regularly. Pages are more static, and the regular parts of your site that stand alone in a separate part of the site.

When you installed WordPress, a page was automatically created for you (along with the first post and first comment). You can see it by clicking on the **About** link under **Pages** in the sidebar:

Adding a page

To add a new page, go to your WP Admin and navigate to **Pages | Add New**, or use the drop-down menu in the top grey menu by clicking on the arrow next to **New Post** and choosing **New Page**. This will take you to the **Add New Page** page:

The minimum you need to do to create a new page is type in a title and some content. Then click on the blue **Publish** button, just as you would for a post, and your new page will appear linked in the sidebar of your website.

You'll recognize most of the fields on this page from the **Add New Post** page, and they work the same for pages as they do for posts. Let's talk about the one new section, the box called **Attributes**.

Parent

WordPress allows you to structure your pages hierarchically. This way, you can organize your website's pages into main pages and subpages, which is useful if you're going to have a lot of pages on your site. For example, if I was writing this blog along with three other authors, we would each have one page about us on the site, but they'd be subpages of the main **About** page. If I was adding one of these pages, I'd choose **About** as the parent page for this new page.

Template

Theme designers often offer alternate templates that can be used for special pages. The default WordPress theme comes with two templates: **Archives** and **Links**. Let's try using the **Archives** template.

Just give your new page a title (for example, **Blog Archives**) and some content (for example, **Let's experiment with the archives template**). Then choose **Archives** from the **Template** pull-down menu and publish your page. When you go to your site and click on the **Blog Archives** link in the sidebar, you'll see this:

As you can see, your title and content both do not appear, which makes this different from pages that use the default template (such as the **About** page that we looked at earlier). The sidebar is also missing. What does appear are the search box, a list of blog archives organized by month, and a list of archives organized by subject, that is, **Categories**.

This particular template doesn't appear useful because all of its information is currently in the sidebar of the rest of the site. However, this shows you the power of a template. If you're designing a theme for your own website, you can create any number of templates that have special content.

The **Links** template creates a similar page, but it lists all of your links. We'll discuss this in more detail later.

Order

By default, the pages in your page list on the sidebar of your blog will be in alphabetical order. If you want them in some other order, you can specify it by entering numbers in the **Order** box for all of your pages. Pages with lower numbers (**0**) will be listed before pages with higher numbers (**5**).

As the WordPress developers acknowledge right on this page, this method of ordering pages is quite clunky. Luckily, there is a plugin that makes ordering pages much easier.

You can download this from `http://wordpress.org/extend/plugins/pagemash/`.

Managing pages

To see a list of all the pages on your website in the WP Admin, navigate to **Pages | Edit** in the main menu. You'll see the **Edit Pages** page:

Title	Author	💬	Date
About Edit | Quick Edit | Delete | View	admin	0	2008/11/20 Published
Blog Archives Edit | Quick Edit | Delete | View	admin	0	14 mins ago Published
Title	Author	💬	Date

By now this list format should begin to look familiar to you. You've got your list of pages, and in each row are a number of useful links allowing you to **Edit**, **Quick Edit**, **Delete**, or **View** the page. You can click on an author's name to filter the list by that author. You can use the two links at the top, **All** and **Published**, to filter the pages by status. And you can check boxes and mass-edit pages by using the **Bulk Actions** menu at the top and bottom of the list. You can also search your pages with the search box at the top.

Links

WordPress gives you a very powerful way of organizing external links or bookmarks on your site. This is a way to link other related blogs—websites you like, websites that you think your visitors will find useful, or just any category of link you want—to your blog. Speaking of categories, you can create and manage link categories that are separate from your blog categories.

When you installed WordPress, it created the link category **Blogroll** along with a number of links in that category. You can see them in your blog's sidebar as follows:

Adding a new link

Let's add a new link to the **Blogroll** category. In your WP Admin, navigate to **Links | Add New**. This will take you to the **Add New Link** page, which has a number of boxes in which you can add information about your new link. Let's look at the first three here:

Of all the fields on this page, it's the top two that are the most important. You need to give your link a **Name**, which is the text people will see and can click on. You also need to give a **Web Address**, which is the URL of the website that is linked to your blog. You can add a description, which will show up when visitors hover over the link. (Alternatively, you can also choose to have the description show up on the page below the link.)

Now let's look at the next two boxes in the following screenshot:

The first box in the screenshot above should look familiar because it's very similar to the **Categories** selection box for posts. Keep in mind that link categories are separate from post categories. On this page, you will only see link categories. You can assign a category to the new link that you're adding or create a brand new category by clicking on the **+ Add New Category** link. Your links will be organized by the categories on your website. The second box lets you choose whether your visitors will be taken to a new window, or a new tab, when they click on the link. I generally recommend always using **_blank** when sending people to an external website.

The other boxes on this page are used less commonly. You can use the two new boxes to specify **XFN (XHTML Friends Network)** relationships between you and any individuals you link to.

Learning more
If you want to learn more about XFN, take a look at this website: http://gmpg.org/xfn/.

The final box at the bottom of this page will allow you to specify:

- An image that belongs with this link (for example, the logo of the company whose site you are linking to)
- The RSS feed for the website you're linking to
- Any notes you have about the site, beyond what you entered into the **Description** box
- A rating for the site from **0** to **9**

To make use of any of these pieces of information, you need to have a theme that recognizes and makes use of them.

At the top right of the page is a **Save** box with a checkbox that you can check if you want to keep the link private, that is, if you don't want it to show up on your site to anyone but you. Click on the **Add Link** button in that box to save your new link.

I added a link for a recipe and food website using this form. I filled in only the first three boxes as seen in this screenshot:

Now when I save and then re-load my website, I see my new link here:

Managing links and categories

You can manage your links just as you manage posts and pages. Navigate to **Links** and you will see this:

From here, you can click on the name of a link to edit it, click on the URL to visit it, and see which categories you've chosen for it. Using the **View all Categories** pull-down menu, you can filter links by categories, change the order, and do bulk deletes.

Just as with post categories, you can manage and add new link categories on the **Link Categories** page. You can access this page by navigating to **Links | Link Categories**:

From this page, you can both add a new category using the form at the left and also manage your existing categories using the table at the right.

Media library

The media library is where WordPress stores all of your uploaded files—images, PDFs, music, video, and so on. To see your media library, navigate to **Media** in the main menu:

This is the now-familiar management table. My media library has only one photo that I uploaded when I posted about the butternut squash soup recipe. As you can see from this table, it shows me the following:

- A thumbnail of the image. If this were another type of media, I'd see an icon representing the type of media.
- The title that I gave the file when I uploaded it, along with the format extension.
- The author.
- Information about which post or page the file is attached to. This will be important when it comes to making an image gallery. The uploaded file will be attached to the post or page that you are editing while uploading a file.
- The number of comments waiting on the attached post or page.
- The date when the file was uploaded.

If you hover over the row with your mouse, links for **Edit**, **Delete**, and **View** will appear. You can click on the file's title or the **Edit** link to edit the **Title**, **Caption**, and **Description**. You cannot edit anything else about uploaded files.

You can also add a new file to your media library. Navigate to **Media | Add New** to get a page similar to the upload media page that you got while uploading a file for a post. When you click on the **Select Files** button and select the file to be uploaded, it will upload it and then give you the options shown in this screenshot:

Enter a title, caption, and description if you want, and click on the **Save all changes** button. Your new item will appear in the media library, which will be unattached to any post or page. However, you'll still be able to use what you just uploaded in any post or page.

To do that, click on the **Upload/Insert** button as you did before. But instead of choosing a file **From Computer**, click on the **Media Library** tab on the top of the box:

When you click on the **Show** link that is next to the image you want to use, you'll get the same set of options you got after uploading an image. Now you can click on the **Insert into Post** button.

Adding an image gallery

You can add an image gallery to any page or post in your website without needing any kind of plugin for WordPress. The following are the simple steps to do this:

1. Choose a post or page for your image gallery.
2. Upload the images you want in that gallery.
3. Add the special code to the page or post, and save it.

Let's get started.

Choosing a post or page

For my food blog, I'm going to create a new page called **My Food Photos** for my image gallery. You can always do this on an existing page or post as well. Here's my new page:

Note where I have left my cursor. I made sure to leave it in a spot on the page where I want my gallery to show up, that is, underneath my introductory text.

Uploading images

Now click on the **Upload/Insert** image icon and upload some photos. Each time you upload a photo, enter the title and then click on the **Save All Changes** button. You'll be taken to the **Gallery** tab, which will show all of the photos you've uploaded to be attached to this page:

If you want to upload more photos at this point, just click on the **From Computer** tab at the top and upload another photo.

When you've uploaded all the photos you want (you can add more later), click on the **Insert gallery** button. This overlay box will disappear and you'll see your post again. The page will have the gallery icon placeholder in the spot where you left the cursor, as seen in this screenshot:

If you're in the HTML view, you'll see the gallery shortcode in that spot:

Note that because I'm uploading these photos while adding/editing this particular page, all of these photos will be "attached" to this page. That's how I know they'll be in the gallery on this page. Any other photos that I've uploaded at other times will not be included. For example, even though I uploaded the Breakfast Shake photo once already, I had to upload it a second time so that it would be attached to this page's gallery.

Now publish or save your page. Now when you view the page, there's a gallery of your images as follows:

Tweaking your gallery

There are a number of tweaks you may want to apply to your gallery.

Adding captions to thumbnails

You may want the captions to show up underneath your thumbnails on the gallery page. To do that, just add captions to the images—go to your media library, edit each image, and give it a caption. The titles that you give the images will show up in the page title.

Changing the size of the images in the gallery

By default, the gallery shows thumbnail versions of your images. If you want, you can change that to be a medium or large version. You just have to edit the gallery shortcode. In your WP Admin, navigate to **Edit Page** for this page (in which we have placed the gallery) and use the **HTML** editing mode instead of **Visual**. Change your gallery shortcode from [gallery] to [gallery size="medium"]. These will be too wide to fit into three columns, so you should change the number of columns to 1. To do this, change your gallery shortcode to this: [gallery size="medium" columns="1"]. Update the page and take another look:

Changing the image page

When you click on one of your thumbnails on the gallery page, you'll be taken to the image page, which shows the medium version of the image along with next and previous thumbnails as follows:

I find this page to be quite unsatisfactory. The main image is too small and the thumbnails are too large. In fact, instead of thumbnails, I'd prefer to use text—that is, just the image titles. Unfortunately, the gallery feature in WordPress is still relatively new, and they haven't made these things easy to change. You *can* change this page to be better, but it requires you to roll up your sleeves and dig into the code a bit.

To change the image size on this page, you have to change the dimensions of your medium images on the **Media Settings** page. (You can access this page by navigating to **Settings | Media**). This change will be applied only to the images you upload after the change. So any images that you've already uploaded will keep their current size unless you delete and re-upload them.

You can find a great explanation for replacing thumbnail navigation links with text links on *Michael Fields'* blog: `http://mfields.org/2008/04/26/adding-text-links-to-wordpress-gallery/`.

Adding plugins

Plugins are little packages of code that you can add to WordPress to increase its functionality. Developers all over the world create plugins, some of which you can use for free, whereas some others are available for purchase.

The steps for installing a plugin are simple:

1. Find your plugin.
2. Download it.
3. Upload and activate it.
4. Configure and/or implement it (if necessary).

Finding your plugin

The best place to find plugins is the WordPress **Plugin Directory** at `http://wordpress.org/extend/plugins/`. There are more plugins every day (as of this writing, there are nearly 4,245) and millions of downloads (22,152,788 and counting). You can search plugins by topic and by tag, as well as see a list of the most popular, newest, and recently updated plugins. This is the best available plugin resource and you should always go here first when looking for a plugin.

You can also do Google searches. I recommend searching for the problem you're trying to solve and see what plugins other users recommend and why. Often, there are multiple plugins that perform similar functions, and you will find the feedback of other WordPress users valuable in choosing between them.

Downloading the plugin

Let's install a plugin that I think everyone should have. It's called **WP-DB-Backup** and it adds the ability to easily create a complete database export of your blog. This offers a more thorough backup than the built-in **Export** function.

You can download the plugin from this page: `http://wordpress.org/extend/plugins/wp-db-backup/`.

Before downloading any plugin, check to see which versions of WordPress the plugin is supposed to work with. If you're downloading a plugin from the `Wordpress.org` website, you'll see everything you need to know on the right side of the page:

This plugin requires Version 2.0.3 or higher and will work with all versions up to 2.7, so we are safe. Now just click on the orange **Download** button and save the resulting ZIP file on your computer where you can find it again.

Uploading and activating the plugin

Unlike with themes, you don't have to unzip the ZIP file. Just go to your WP Admin and navigate to **Plugins | Add New**. There are a lot of things on this page, but just look for the **Install a plugin in .zip format** section:

Browse to your plugin and then click on the **Install Now** button.

If the installation is successful, you'll get a page telling you that the installation was successful and giving you the option to activate the plugin right from this page:

Click on the **Activate Plugin** link and you're done activating your plugin.

If this automatic uploader *doesn't* work for you, you can do this the old-fashioned way:

First extract the ZIP file you downloaded so that it's a folder, probably called `wp-db-backup`.

Using your FTP client, upload this folder inside the `wp-content/plugins/` folder of your WordPress installation. You'll also see the two plugins that WordPress came with in that folder—**akismet** and **hello.php**.

Now go to your WP Admin and navigate to **Plugins | Installed**. You'll see the three plugins on this page. Just click on the **Activate** link in the **WordPress Database Backup** row:

WordPress Database Backup	2.2.1	On-demand backup of your WordPress database. Navigate to Manage → Backup to get started. By Austin Matzko.	Activate	Edit

Now you are ready for the final step, which is to actually make use of this plugin.

Configuring and/or implementing—if necessary

In the case of this plugin, all you have to do is use it. You'll have a new link in your menu that you can navigate to. It's **Tools | Backup**. When you go to this page, you'll be able to choose which tables to back up. If you've installed any plugins that add additional tables, you'll have the option to choose them as well; I always do. I also always check the two boxes to exclude spam comments and post revisions.

You can now decide if you want to save the backup to your server, download it, or have it emailed to you. I suggest downloading it every time.

There is also an option to schedule regular backups. This is not 100% reliable, so you should probably set up a reminder to check if your backup has been emailed to you or not. The frequency you choose should depend on how often you edit your site—once a week is probably often enough for most people.

Scheduled Backup

Schedule:

- Never
- Once Hourly
- Twice Daily
- Once Daily
- Once Weekly

Email backup to: april@springthistle.com

(Schedule backup)

For other plugins, the configure and/or implementation step may be different.

- You may not have to do anything. Some plugins simply change the way WordPress does some things, and activating them is all you need to do.

- You may have to configure a plugin's details before it begins to work. Some plugins need you to make choices and set new settings.

- There may not be a configuration page, but you may have to add some code to one of your theme's template files.

If you're unsure of what to do after you've uploaded and activated your plugin, be sure to read the `readme` file that came with your plugin, or look at the **Faq** on the plugin's website.

Many plugin authors accept donations. I strongly recommend giving donations to the authors of plugins that you find useful. It helps to encourage everyone in the community to continue writing great plugins that everyone can use.

Auto-installation

The newest version of WordPress, as of 2.7, offers a way for you to search for, choose, and install new plugins directly through your WP Admin interface. You can do this by using the **Search** area on the **Plugins | Add New** page. If you already know what plugin you want, you can type it in and follow the onscreen instructions. I still recommend that you do your research carefully to be sure that you find the plugin that you want and that it's compatible with your version of WordPress. Also, although most of the great plugins are on Wordpress.org, there are still more that can be found elsewhere on the Web. So be sure to do a thorough search.

Summary

This chapter explored all of the content WordPress can manage that's not directly about blogging. You learned about static pages, bookmark links, the media library, image galleries, plugins, and more.

You are now fully equipped to use the WordPress Admin panel to control all of your website's content. Next, you'll want to control the display. In the next chapter we will start discussing themes.

5
Choosing and Installing Themes

One of the greatest advantages of using a **CMS (Content Management System)** for your blog or website is that you are able to change the look and feel of your website without knowing how to code in HTML and CSS. Almost every CMS allow users to change the look of their site without having to worry about their content being changed. These managed looks are called **themes**. On other platforms (such as Blogger), themes are called **templates** or **layouts**.

Thousands of WordPress themes are available for download free of cost. These themes are developed by members of the WordPress community and listed in a separate area of WordPress's main website (`http://wordpress.org/extend/themes/`).

Before you decide to use any particular theme, you will want to know:

- Some basic things about the theme
- How to install a theme
- How to choose the theme that best suits your content and audience
- How to modify static content inside these themes

In this chapter we will discuss all of these topics. This chapter is a ground-up guide to using themes. In the next chapter, we will discuss the advanced topic of developing your own themes.

> If you are using WordPress.com to host your WordPress website, you cannot upload themes to your site; you have to choose from the themes that WordPress.com makes available to you. So you can skip forward to the *Previewing and Activating* section of this chapter.

Finding themes

There are many different websites you can search to find themes available for download. Many theme developers offer their themes for free, whereas some charge a small fee. Of course, if you cannot find a free theme that fits your needs, you can always hire a theme developer to create a customized theme for you, or you can be your own theme developer (see Chapter 6).

WordPress Theme Directory

The first place you should always go to when looking for a theme is the official WordPress **Theme Directory** at `http://wordpress.org/extend/themes/`. This is where everyone in the WordPress community uploads their free themes and tags them with keywords that describe the basic look, layout, and function of their theme. Look at this screenshot:

By looking at the list of popular themes on the right, you can see which themes are chosen most often.

To get a better idea of what a theme will look like than what's offered by the thumbnail, just click on the title of the theme. You'll be taken to the theme's detail page:

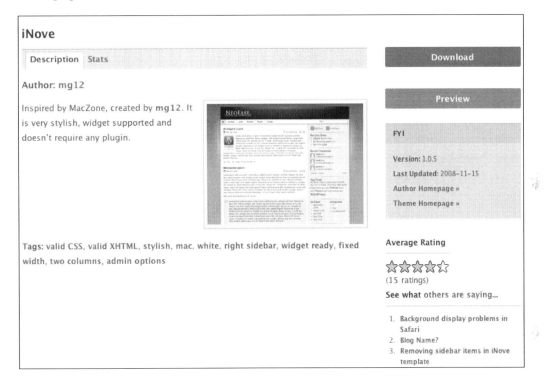

This page shows you the theme's description, all of the tags that apply to it, the average rating given to it by other users, and some comments on the theme. If you click on the **Preview** button, you'll get to see the theme actually in action.

The theme in action will look like this:

This preview is very useful. It not only shows you exactly what the theme will look like and what is included in the sidebar, but also includes examples of a variety of different HTML and styleable elements so that you can see how they'll look. These elements include:

- Images
- Headings (1, 2, 3, 4, 5, and 6)
- Paragraphs
- Lists
- Forms
- Tables

- Blockquote
- Code
- Links

If you browse around this site and find a theme you like, just click on the **Download** link for that theme and it'll download a zipped theme file to your computer.

To extract the files from the ZIP file, use your computer's built-in unzipping utility or download WinZip.

Top WP themes

Another great place to look for themes is `http://topwpthemes.com/`. This site provides essentially the same service as the WordPress Theme Directory, but they have a different collection of themes from a restricted number of designers and they also have some advertising on the site. Have a look at this screenshot:

Just like the WordPress Theme Directory, on this site you can preview a theme and download a ZIP file to your computer.

Template Monster

If you can't find a free theme that you want to use, you can always consider buying a theme. Most commercial themes are offered at two prices. The first price is simply the cost of buying the theme for your own use and is usually around $40 to $45. The second price is the price you pay if you want to be the only user of the theme and that can be anywhere from $500 to $1,500.

Template Monster, `http://templatemonster.com`, is a big seller of all kinds of templates and designs. They have a whole section devoted to WordPress Themes (which they mistakenly refer to as **WordPress Templates** in some places):

When you find a theme you like on Template Monster, you can preview it in **LIVE DEMO** just as you can on the WordPress Theme Directory site. Also, you can customize it before purchase. When you're ready, you just pay the fee and then download the theme as you would from one of the free sites.

Finding more themes

These are by no means the only sites that offer a large gallery of theme options! Just do a Google search for "WordPress themes" and you'll get over six million hits. Also, keep in mind that you can choose a basic theme now and customize it or create your own from scratch later as you build skills by reading this book.

Factors to consider when choosing a theme

As you look through all of the available themes, you'll see that there is quite a variety of both look and feel, and layout. When considering a theme, make sure to ask yourself the following questions:

- Do I like the design of the header?
- Does the sidebar display the information I want (for example, categories, pages, tags, links, and so on)?
- Is it complex or simple?
- Does it have two columns or three columns?

If you choose a widget-ready theme, some of these issues will be moot.

Installing and changing themes

Now that you've chosen the theme you want to use, you'll need to install it into your WordPress website. In the following sections, we'll look at a brief overview of what a theme actually is, and go through the steps to upload and activate a theme on your WordPress website.

What makes a theme?

A WordPress **theme** is actually a collection of files in a folder. There are no special or unusual formats, just a few requirements for those files in the theme folder. The only requirements for a folder to be a valid WordPress theme are:

1. It should have a `style.css` file and an `index.php` file.

2. The `style.css` file must have the basic theme information in its first five lines.

There are a number of additional files that you'll find in most theme folders. They are:

- A `screenshot.png` file — this is the little thumbnail that shows what the theme looks like

- An `images` folder — this is where all images associated with the theme live

- A variety of files that are used for different purposes (for example, `header.php`, `footer.php`, `page.php`, `single.php`, `archive.php`, and so on)

You don't have to worry about these details now, but knowing them will help you identify what is going on in the themes you download for now. This will also be useful in the next chapter when we discuss making your own theme from scratch.

When you download a theme, you are actually just downloading a zipped folder.

Downloading and extracting

Once you find a theme that you want to use, download it to your computer, to your desktop for example. When this is done, you'll see a ZIP file on your desktop (for example, `corporate.1.3.5.zip`). If you're using Mac, the ZIP file may have automatically been unzippped for you, in which case you'll see a folder on your desktop as well (for example, `corporate`). If not, then just do the extraction/unzipping manually so that you have the theme folder on your desktop.

These are the file contents of the corporate folder that I downloaded:

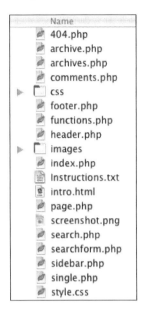

It's got a `style.css` file and an `index.php` file, and so I know it's definitely a valid theme.

Uploading the theme

Now you need to upload the theme folder to your WordPress website. As you did in Chapter 2, you need to FTP to your server. Once there, navigate to your WordPress website's installation folder. Next, go to the `wp-content` folder and then to the `themes` folder. You'll see two theme folders in here already: `classic` and `default`. These are the two themes that come pre-installed with WordPress.

Upload the folder you just unzippped (for example, `corporate`) into the `themes` folder on your server. Now that I've uploaded the theme I chose, **Corporate**, it shows up in the themes folder along with the two default themes as follows:

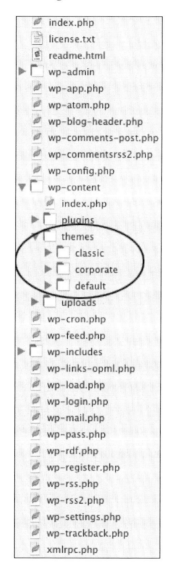

Previewing and activating

For the next step, you need to log in to the WP Admin (by going to
`http://yoursite.com/wp-admin`) and navigate to **Appearance**. This will
take you to the main **Manage Themes** page in the admin panel:

This page shows you, under **Current Theme**, information about the theme you are
currently using. This includes the theme's title, designer, version, and details. Below
that, under **Available Themes**, it shows you all of the available themes you have in
your WordPress installation. I've got just the three themes we saw in the file list on
my server: **Classic**, **Default**, and the new one I just uploaded—**Corporate**.

Whenever you add a new theme in the themes folder, you will find it on this page. If
you upload a defective theme, it will show up in a new list at the bottom of the page
with a note saying that the theme is missing some required information.

When you click on the thumbnail of any of the available themes, you'll get a preview of what it will look like on your site. When I click on **Corporate**, I see this:

A preview of my own content within the new theme shows up here. It's not activated yet; this is just my chance to be sure everything looks right. If I like it, I can just click on the **Activate "Corporate"** link at the top right. If I don't like it, I can click on the little **x** at the top left. Once I activate it, **Corporate** becomes my selected theme. When you activate your new theme and point your browser to your WordPress website, you'll see that the new theme has been applied.

You can even install a plugin that lets users switch between installed themes. You can get it here: http://plugins.trac.wordpress.org/wiki/ThemeSwitcher.

Using widgets

Widgets, also known as "sidebar accessories," are a useful tool that allows you to personalize what shows up in your sidebar(s) without having to write any PHP or HTML code. You can add design elements, content, images, gadgets, and more.

 If you want to use widgets with your website, you have to be sure you have a widgets-ready theme. Not all themes are capable of using widgets. If you're browsing through themes on `WordPress.org`, you'll see that some themes have the tag "widgets" or "widgets-ready." You must choose from these themes to be able to use widgets.

Widgets come as a part of your WordPress installation as of WordPress 2.2. For earlier versions of WordPress, widgets were available as a plugin.

Enabling basic widgets

When you first install your theme, you'll notice that it comes with some elements in the sidebar by default. For example, in the theme I chose, the sidebar shows **Pages**, **Archives**, **Categories**, **Blogroll**, and **Meta**.

Pages

About

Archives

November 2008

Categories

Uncategorized

Blogroll

Development Blog
Documentation
Plugins
Suggest Ideas
Support Forum
Themes
WordPress Planet

Meta

Log out
Site Feed
Comments Feed

What if I don't want the theme designer to be able to choose the content of my sidebar? All I have to do is choose what I want in the sidebar by using widgets.

In your WP Admin, navigate to **Appearance | Widgets**:

As soon as I add just one widget to my sidebar, all of the default elements in the sidebar that came with the theme will disappear. For example, let's say I want to have a search box in the sidebar. All I have to do is click on the **Add** link next to **Search**. A **Search** bar will appear on the right under **Current Widgets**, as shown in this screenshot:

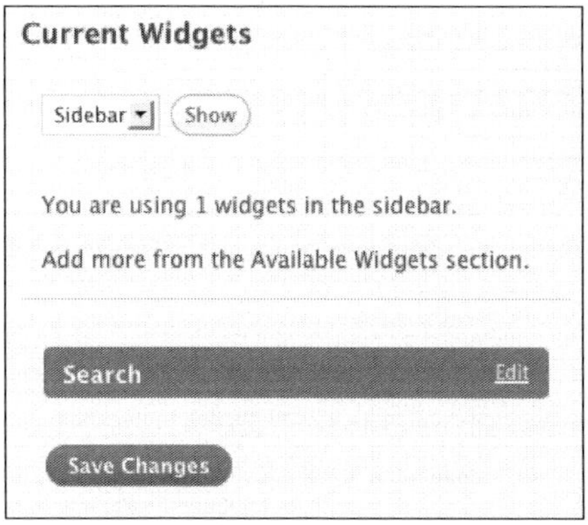

Current Widgets

Sidebar ▾ (Show)

You are using 1 widgets in the sidebar.

Add more from the Available Widgets section.

Search   Edit

Save Changes

Now I can click on **Save Changes** and go back to my website. Now my sidebar has changed to this:

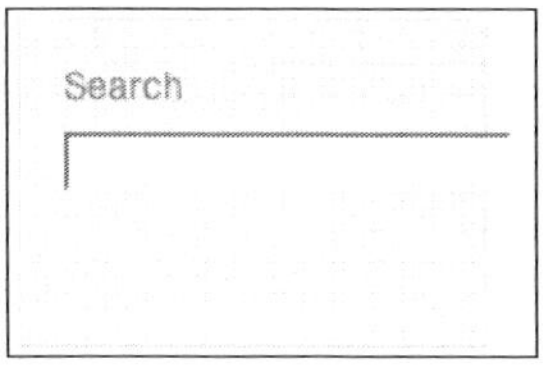

Search

I can add as many more widgets to my sidebar as I want. Also, most widgets have a variety of options that you can set. For example, take a look at the widgets **Pages** and **Categories**. When you click on **Add**, the widgets show up at the right under **Current Widgets**. You can click on the **Edit** link in the bar, which will open up the widget's options:

Current Widgets

Sidebar ▾ | (Show)

You are using 3 widgets in the sidebar.

Add more from the Available Widgets section.

| Search | Edit |

| Pages | Cancel |

Title:

Learn More

Sort by:

Page order ▾

Exclude:

Page IDs, separated by commas.

(Done)   (Remove)

| Categories | Cancel |

Title:

Categories

☐ Show as dropdown
☑ Show post counts
☐ Show hierarchy

(Done)   (Remove)

Save Changes

I've chosen a title for my pages listing and want to display them sorted by page order. Moreover, I could exclude any pages from the list if I wanted. I've also chosen a title for my list of categories as well as the option to show post counts. When I click on the **Done** button for both widgets and then click on **Save Changes**, I can revisit my live sidebar and see that my new widgets are active:

Multiple sidebars

The **Corporate** theme we are looking at has just one sidebar. It's called **Sidebar** and shows up as the only item in the pull-down menu under **Current Widgets**, as follows:

Some widget-ready themes will have multiple sidebars and they will be listed in this menu. For example, the iNove theme has the following four sidebars:

To add widgets to a different sidebar (that is, other than the default or first sidebar), choose the sidebar you want to add widgets to and then click on the **Show** button. This will switch your view to the sidebar you've chosen. Now you can see which widgets that sidebar already has and you can add more widgets to it.

Once you've chosen your theme, you can investigate the widgets page to see how the theme developer set up the sidebars for widgets.

Adding new widgets

The widgets that come pre-installed with your WordPress installation are not the only widgets available to you. Just like themes, widgets are developed by people in the WordPress community and made available online.

The central website for finding new widgets is `http://widgets.wordpress.com`. The widgets on this site are organized into such categories as **Humor**, **Discussion**, **Income**, **Links**, **Utility**, **Random**, and so on.

If you find a widget on this website that you like, you can download it, unzip it, and upload it very similarly to the way you got your new theme. Once you've done that, it'll show up in the list of available widgets on the **Widgets** page of your WP Admin.

> **Hot tip**: If you want to put any HTML code in the blog and cannot find the widget for it, just paste it in a Text widget. This will usually work.

Summary

This chapter describes how to manage the basic look of your WordPress website. You have learned where to find themes, why they are useful, and how to implement new themes on your WordPress website.

You also learned how to use widgets to personalize the content of your website's sidebar.

In the next chapter, you will learn, step-by-step, how to build your own theme from scratch.

6
Developing Your Own Theme

You know how to find themes on the Web and install them for use on your WordPress site. But you may not be able to find the perfect theme, or you may want to create a thoroughly personalized theme, or you may be a website designer with a client who wants a custom theme.

In this chapter you'll learn how to turn your own design into a fully functional WordPress theme that you'll be able to use on your own site. You'll also learn how to convert your theme folder into a ZIP file that can be shared with other WordPress users on the Web.

All you will need before we get started is:

- Your own design
- The ability to slice and dice your design to turn it into HTML

We'll start out with tips on slicing and dicing so that your HTML and CSS files are as WordPress-friendly as possible, and then cover the steps for turning that HTML build into a fully functional theme.

Note that I assume that you are already comfortable writing and working with HTML and CSS. You do not need to be familiar with PHP because I'll be walking you through all of the PHP code.

Setting up your design

Just about any design in the world can be turned into a WordPress theme. However, there are some general guidelines you can follow—both in the design and the HTML/CSS build of your theme—which will make the design fit very easily into the WordPress theme box.

Designing your theme to be WordPress-friendly

While you can design your blog any way that you want, a good way to start would be with one of the standard blog layouts.

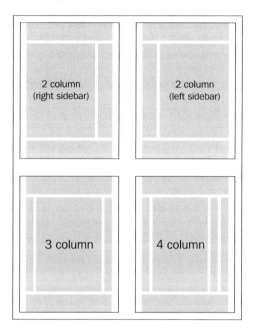

Note that while these different standard layouts have differing numbers of columns and column widths, they all have these essential parts:

- Header
- Main column
- Side column(s)
- Footer

WordPress expects your theme to follow this pattern, and so it provides functions that make it easier to create a theme that has this pattern. As you're designing your first blog theme, I suggest including these parts. Also, a design that stays within the same general design patterns of WordPress themes will most easily accommodate existing plugins and widgets.

The two-column layout is the simplest and the easiest to implement as a WordPress theme. So, we'll be using this layout as an example in this chapter. This is a screenshot of the design I created in Photoshop for my food blog:

Note that this layout has a header, main column, side column, and footer:

Now that the design is complete, we're ready for the next step: turning the design into code.

Converting your design to code

The next step towards turning your ideal design into a WordPress theme is to slice images out of your design and write HTML and CSS files that put it all together. For the purpose of this chapter, I assume that you already know how to do this in general. We'll cover the ways you can do your slicing and dicing, but in a different way so that your HTML will be best suited for WordPress.

 If you are interested in the details of both designing a theme and slicing it for WordPress, I highly recommend the book *"WordPress Theme Design"*, *Packt Publishing, 9781847193094* by Tessa Blakeley Silver. This book minutely covers topics such as choosing a color scheme, considering typography, writing the best CSS, and laying out your HTML using Rapid Design Comping.

My HTML build folder, which has my HTML, CSS, and image files, looks like this:

```
▼  ☐ HTML build
   ▶  ☐ images
      📄 index.html
      📝 style.css
```

We will now take a look at some of the choices I made when writing these HTML and CSS files so that you can take advantage of these tips and tricks.

Examining the HTML structure

Here is the very basic (not final) layout of my HTML file for my food blog design:

```
<!DOCTYPE html PUBLIC "-//W3C//DTD XHTML 1.0 Transitional//EN"
"http://www.w3.org/TR/xhtml1/DTD/xhtml1-transitional.dtd">
<html xmlns="http://www.w3.org/1999/xhtml">
<head>
    <title>Blog title</title>
    <style type="text/css">@import url("style.css");</style>
</head>
<body>

<div id="container">
    <div id="header">
        <div id="mainnav">
```

```
        <ul>
            <li>Navigation list item</li>
        </ul>
    </div><!-- /mainnav -->
    <h1><a href="#">My Blog Title</a></h1>
    <div id="description">this is My subtitle</div>
</div><!-- /header -->

<div id="content">
    <div id="copy">
        <div class="post">
            <h2><a href="#">Post Title</a></h2>
            <div class="post-date">Post Date</div>
            <p>Post Content</p>
            <div class="categories">Categories</div>
            <div class="tags">Tags</div>
            <div class="comments">Comments</div>
        </div>
    </div>
    <div id="sidebar">
        <h3>Categories</h3>
        <ul>
            <li>category list item</li>
        </ul>
        <h3>Archives</h3>
        <ul>
            <li>archive list item</li>
        </ul>
    </div><!-- /sidebar -->
</div><!-- /content -->

<div id="footer">
    Footer text
</div><!-- /footer -->
</div><!-- /container -->

</body>
</html>
```

You can see that I've separated out these four major parts:

- The header is in the div with id="header"
- The side column is in the div with id="sidebar"
- The main column is in the div with id="copy"
- The footer is in the div with id="footer"

I'd like to call your attention to a few other things I've done here:

- The `mainnav` is in an unordered list (`ul`)

  I did this because WordPress has a function that spits out the pages of your site in the order you choose. When WordPress spits out the list, every linked page title is in a list item tag (`li`).

- **Archives** and **Categories** are similar

  There are going to be a number of items that you may want to add to your sidebar, including widgets. Many of these items will be lists with titles, so I've prepared for that in my HTML.

- Within the `div id="copy"` is a `div` with the `class="post"`

  Even though this basic layout has just one post in it, I know that I'll want to show more than one post at a time. I've created this `div` expecting that it'll be repeated for each post. Also, WordPress expects this `div` to be called `"post"`. (We'll get into that later.)

Now that I've got my basic layout, I'm going to add a few more HTML elements to flesh it out a bit, including more information in the `<head>` as well as the search box, and some additional CSS. Then I'll fill up the sidebar, header, content, and footer with bunch of dummy text so that it looks almost exactly like my theme's design in Photoshop. I'm not including the complete HTML here, but you can find it in the code bundle for this chapter (in the folder called `HTML_build`) if you'd like to do the same. However, note that I've left most of the text a little different. This is my trick to remind myself, later, to replace the static text with dynamic WordPress-generated text.

Examining the CSS

Let's now take a look at the CSS. First, we'll review the CSS that displays everything you see in the design. Note that I've got styles for my five key parts: header, sidebar, copy, post, and footer. They are as follows:

```css
body {
    margin: 0px;
    background: #ddd url('images/bg-body.gif') repeat-x;
    font-family:  "Trebuchet MS", Helvetica, Arial, sans-serif;
    font-size: 14px;
}

a, a:visited {
    color: #397cc6;
    text-decoration: none;
}

a:hover {
    text-decoration: underline;
}

/*** STRUCTURAL PLACEMENT - - - - - - - - - - - - - - - - - - - - - */

#container {
    margin: 0 auto;
    width: 837px
}

#header {
    margin: 35px 0 0 0;
    height: 343px;
    background: url('images/header.jpg') no-repeat;
}

#mainnav {
    padding: 40px 0 0 30px;
}

#content {
    background: #fff url('images/bg-content.gif');
    padding: 0 10px 0 10px;
}

#copy {
    width: 590px;
    float: right;
}

#sidebar {
    width: 200px;
```

```
        float: left;
        background-color: #F7F7F7;
}

#footer {
    background: url('images/footer.gif') no-repeat;
    height: 79px;
}

/*** STYLING PIECES - - - - - - - - - - - - - - - - - - - - - - - - - */

/* header title */
#header h1 {
    color: #fff;
    font-size: 24px;
    font-weight: normal;
    margin: 140px 0 5px 500px;
    text-transform: lowercase;
}

#header h1 a {
    color: #fff;
    text-decoration: none;
}

#header h1 a:hover {
    background-color: #9A8A71;
}

#header #description {
    color: #fff;
    margin: 0 0 5px 500px;
    text-transform: lowercase;
}

/* main (top) navigation */
#mainnav ul {
    margin: 0;
    padding: 0;
}

#mainnav li {
    margin: 0;
    padding: 0 30px 0 0;
    display: inline;
    color: #82aedf;
}

#mainnav ul li:before {
    content: "\00A4 \0020 \0020";
```

```
}
#mainnav a, #mainnav a:visited {
    color: #bad2ee;
    text-transform: uppercase;
    text-decoration: none;
}
#mainnav a:hover {
    text-decoration: underline;
}

/* sidebar */
#sidebar {
    padding: 0 0 20px 0;
}
#sidebar h3 {
    color: #b7b6b6;
    font-weight: normal;
    font-size: 18px;
    margin: 30px 0 5px 10px;
}
#sidebar h3.first {
    margin-top: 0;
}
#sidebar ul {
    margin: 0 0 0 10px;
    padding: 0;
}
#sidebar li {
    margin: 0;
    padding: 0;
    list-style-type: none;
}
#sidebar input {
    background-color: #ededed;
    border: 1px solid #ccc;
    padding: 4px;
    margin-left: 10px;
}
/* posts */
.post {
    border-bottom: 3px solid #f7f7f7;
    padding: 0 0 15px 0;
```

```
    }
    .post h2 {
      color: #c1ae90;
      font-weight: normal;
      margin: 0;
    }
    .post h2 a {
      color: #c1ae90;
    }
    .post .categories, .post .tags, .post .post-date {
      color: #bababa;
      font-size: 12px;
    }
    .post .post-date {
      float: right;
      margin-top: -18px;
    }
    .post .comments {
      font-size: 12px;
      float: right;
      margin-top: -20px;
    }
    .post .comments a, .post .comments a:visited {
      background: url('images/icon-comments.gif') no-repeat 0 3px;
      padding: 1px 0 1px 18px;
    }
    .post img {
      padding: 5px;
      border: 4px solid #e2e2e2;
    }
    /* footer */
    #footer {
      color: #dedede;
      font-size: 20px;
      text-align: center;
      padding-top: 20px;
      text-transform: lowercase;
    }
    #footer a, #footer a:visited {
      color: #dedede;
    }
    #footer a:hover {
      color: #bbb;
    }
```

But beyond this, there are some other styles we should add. When WordPress spits out items that include page lists, category lists, archive lists, images, galleries, and so on, it gives many of these items a particular class name. If you know these class names, you can prepare your stylesheet to take advantage of them.

When you add an image to a post or page, WordPress gives you the option to have it to the right, left, or at the centre of the text. Depending on what you choose, WordPress will have the image styled as `alignleft`, `alignright`, or `aligncenter`. Let's add `alignleft` and `alignright` to the stylesheet:

```
/* WordPress styles */
.alignright {
    float: right;
}

.alignleft {
    float: left;
}
```

A class is another necessity for the images that WordPress uses when you add an image with a caption. There are three essential entries you'll want to make in your stylesheet to style the caption box, which are:

```
.wp-caption {
    padding-top: 5px;
    border: 4px solid #e2e2e2;
    text-align: center;
    background-color: #fff;
    margin: 10px;
}
.wp-caption img {
    margin: 0;
    padding: 0;
    border: 0 none;
}
.wp-caption p.wp-caption-text {
    font-size: 11px;
    line-height: 17px;
    padding: 0 4px 5px;
    margin: 0;
}
```

I've designed my caption box to match my captionless images that I styled in `.post img`.

Another frequently used class is `current_page_item`. On the page you are currently working, WordPress adds this to the list item in the pages menu. This gives you the ability to visually mark a page that the user is currently viewing. I'll mark it with an underline using the following code:

```
#mainnav .current_page_item a, #mainnav .current_page_item a:visited {
    text-decoration: underline;
}
```

WordPress uses many other classes that you can take advantage of when building your stylesheet. I've listed a few of them in Chapter 11.

Now that you've got your HTML and CSS lined up, you're ready for the next step: turning the HTML build into a WordPress theme.

Converting your build into a theme

You'll be turning your HTML build into a theme, which is composed of a number of template files and other scripts. We are going to first dig into the inner workings of a theme so as to get familiar with how it's put together. Then we'll actually turn the HTML build into a theme folder that WordPress can use. And finally, we'll replace the dummy text in your build with WordPress functions that spit out content.

Creating the theme folder

The first step to turning your HTML build into a theme is to create your theme folder and give it everything it needs to be recognized as a theme by WordPress. Let's look at an overview of the steps and then take them one by one:

1. Name your folder and create backup copies of your build files.
2. Prepare the essential files.
3. Add a screenshot of your theme called `screenshot.png`.
4. Upload your folder.
5. Activate your theme.

Let's take these steps one by one now:

1. Name your folder and make backup copies.

    You'll want to give your build folder a sensible name. I'm naming my theme **Muffin Top** because of the muffins in my header image. I'll name the folder `muffintop`.

Now I suggest creating backup copies of your HTML and CSS files. As you'll eventually be breaking up your build into template files, you can easily lose track of where your code came from. By keeping a copy of your original build, you'll be able to go back to them for reference.

2. Prepare the essential files.

    WordPress has only the following two requirements to recognize your folder as a theme:

    - A file called `index.php`
    - A file called `style.css` with an introductory comment

    Just re-name `index.html` to `index.php` and that takes care of the first requirement.

    To satisfy the second requirement, your stylesheet needs to have an introductory comment that describes the basic information for the whole theme: title, author, and so on. Also, it has to be at the very top of the stylesheet. I've added this comment to my `style.css` file.

    ```
    /*
    Theme Name: Muffin Top
    Theme URI: http://springthistle.com/wordpress/projects
    Description: Design created especially for April's Food Blog for
        WordPress Complete.
    Version: 1.0
    Author: April Hodge Silver
    Author URI: http://springthistle.com/
    Tags: brown, fixed width, two columns, widgets, food
    */
    ```

    When you add this comment section to your stylesheet, just replace all of the details with those that are relevant to your theme.

3. Add a screenshot.

    Remember when we first learned how to activate a new theme that there were thumbnail versions of the themes in your **Appearance** tab? You'll want a thumbnail of your own design. It has to be a PNG file and with the name `screenshot.png`. Just do the following:

    - Flatten your design in Photoshop.
    - Change the image size to 300px.
    - **Save for web** as a PNG-8.
    - Name your file `screenshot.png` and save it in your build folder.

Now that I've got my theme ready to upload, my theme folder looks like this:

4. Upload your folder.

    Using your FTP software, upload your template folder to `wp-content/themes/` in your WordPress build. It will share the `themes` folder with `default` and `classic` (and any other themes you've added since you installed WordPress). In the next image, you can see my **muffintop** theme (highlighted) living in the **themes** folder:

5. Activate your theme.

    You've got the absolute basic necessities in there now, so you can activate your theme (though it won't look like much yet). Log in to your WP Admin and navigate to **Appearance**. There you'll see your theme waiting for you.

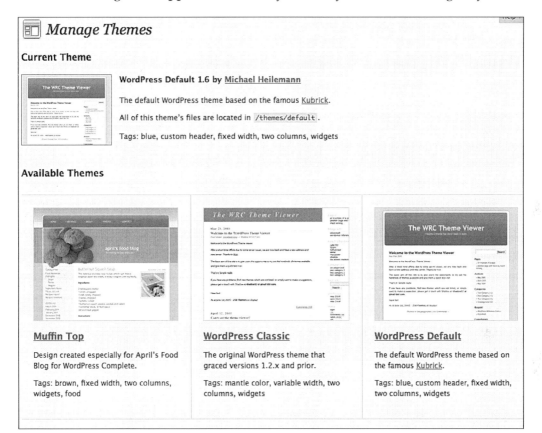

When you click on the thumbnail or theme title of your theme, an overlay window will appear on top of the page with a preview of what your site will look like. Don't be alarmed if it's not perfect. The stylesheet is not yet being pulled in correctly.

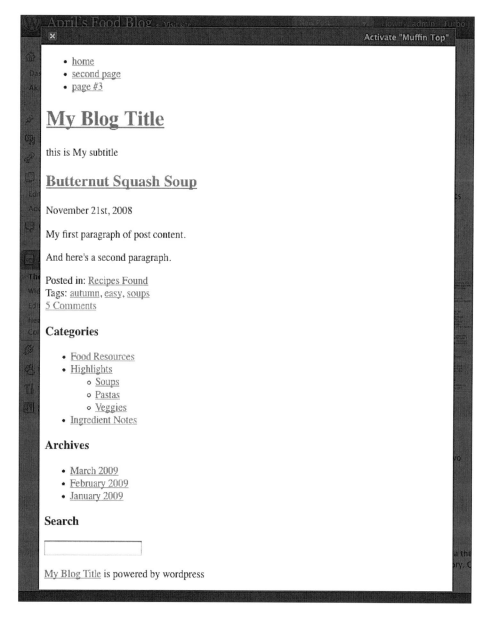

Click on the link in the upper-right corner to activate your theme. This is another good reason to have a development server. You wouldn't want to have this incomplete theme active on a live site while you finish the final pieces!

Speaking of final pieces, your theme is now ready to have all of the WordPress content added.

Adding WordPress content

Right now, your `index.php` file is your only theme file. We'll be breaking it up into template files a bit later. First, we need to replace the dummy text with WordPress functions that will spit out your actual content into your theme.

The <head> tag

First we'll set up the `<head></head>` section of your HTML file. Let's start with the stylesheet. WordPress provides a function that knows where your stylesheet lives. Replace the code `style.css` in your `index.php` file with this:

```
<?php bloginfo('stylesheet_url'); ?>
```

Using this function instead of a hardcoded call to the stylesheet will come in handy if you ever have a need to re-name your theme folder. Now when you look at your site, you see your theme, along with the dummy text, in all its glory.

You need to add another important chunk of code to put header tags into your theme for the RSS feed, the Atom feed, the **pingback** URL, and other miscellaneous WordPress stuff. Add these three lines in your `<head>` section:

```
<link rel="alternate"
      type="application/rss+xml"
      title="<?php bloginfo('name'); ?> RSS Feed"
      href="<?php bloginfo('rss2_url'); ?>" />
<link rel="alternate"
      type="application/atom+xml"
      title="<?php bloginfo('name'); ?> Atom Feed"
      href="<?php bloginfo('atom_url'); ?>" />
<link rel="pingback"
      href="<?php bloginfo('pingback_url'); ?>" />
```

And add this line right before the closing `</head>` tag:

```
<?php wp_head(); ?>
```

Finally, you'll want WordPress to be able to place your blog's name in the title bar of your browser. So replace your dummy title with this code in the title tag:

```
<?php wp_title('&laquo;', true, 'right'); ?>
<?php bloginfo('name'); ?>
```

This will spit out the title of the current page, then an arrow, and then the title of your blog. Your header now looks something like this:

```
<head>
    <title><?php wp_title('&laquo;', true, 'right'); ?>
        <?php bloginfo('name'); ?></title>
    <meta name="robots"
        content="index, follow"></meta>
    <meta name="distribution"
        content="global"></meta>
    <meta name="description"
        content="discovering new recipes and food daily"></meta>
    <meta name="keywords"
        content="april hodge silver, food, recipes"></meta>
    <style type="text/css">
     @import url("<?php bloginfo('stylesheet_url'); ?>");
    </style>
    <link rel="alternate"
        type="application/rss+xml"
        title="<?php bloginfo('name'); ?> RSS Feed"
        href="<?php bloginfo('rss2_url'); ?>" />
    <link rel="alternate"
        type="application/atom+xml"
        title="<?php bloginfo('name'); ?> Atom Feed"
        href="<?php bloginfo('atom_url'); ?>" />
    <link rel="pingback"
        href="<?php bloginfo('pingback_url'); ?>" />
    <?php wp_head(); ?>
</head>
```

The header and footer

It's time to start adding the content that you can see. Let's first replace the dummy text in the main navigation bar and header with WordPress content tags.

WordPress will generate a linked list of pages for you, as I mentioned earlier. Just replace your dummy text with this useful tag, placing it inside the <ul></ul> tag:

```
<?php wp_list_pages('title_li=' ); ?>
```

The reason for the title_li= part is that by default this function will add a title to your list of pages. In this case, I don't want it and so I have to declare it blank.

Next, you can replace your dummy blog title and dummy blog description with the following two tags:

```
<?php bloginfo('name'); ?>
<?php bloginfo('description'); ?>
```

These tags pull information from where you set the blog name and description in the WP Admin, and you can simply change them from the **Settings | General** page.

And finally, if you want to link the blog title in the header to the homepage of the blog, use this for the URL:

```
<?php echo get_option('home'); ?>/
```

Now the part of your HTML that describes the header looks like this:

```
<div id="header">
    <div id="mainnav">
        <ul>
            <?php wp_list_pages('title_li=' ); ?>
        </ul>
    </div><!-- /mainnav -->
    <h1>
        <a href="<?php echo get_option('home'); ?>/">
            <?php bloginfo('name'); ?></a>
    </h1>
    <div id="description"><?php bloginfo('description'); ?></div>
</div><!-- /header -->
```

Are you wondering why you should bother with some of this when you could have just typed your blog title, URL, and description to the theme? One reason is that if you ever want to change your blog's title, you can just do it in one quick step in the WP Admin and it will change all over your site. The other reason is that if you want to share your theme with others, you'll need to give them the ability to easily change the name through their own WP Admin panel.

Now when I refresh the site, my dummy text in the header has been replaced with actual content from my blog:

Just to tie things up, I'm going to add the same code to my footer for displaying the home URL and blog title. My footer section now looks like this:

```
<div id="footer">
    <a href="<?php echo get_option('home'); ?>/">
        <?php bloginfo('name'); ?></a> is powered by wordpress
</div><!-- /footer -->
```

The sidebar

Now we can move along to adding WordPress-generated content in the sidebar, which still has just the dummy text:

Categories

Food Resources
Highlights
  Soups
  Pastas
  Veggies
Ingredient Notes

Archives

March 2009
February 2009
January 2009

Search

Starting at the top, replace your dummy text for the list of categories with the following WordPress categories tag. Again, be sure to place it within the `<ul></ul>` tag.

```
<?php wp_list_categories('title_li='); ?>
```

Just like with pages, you need to turn off the default title by using `title_li=`.

Now, replace your dummy text for the list of archives with this tag:

```
<?php wp_get_archives(); ?>
```

The next item down, the search, is also a simple matter of pasting in the WordPress code. In this case, it's a relatively new function:

```
<?php get_search_form(); ?>
```

Now, the part of your HTML that describes the sidebar looks something like this:

```
<div id="sidebar">
    <h3 class="first">Categories</h3>
    <ul>
        <?php wp_list_categories('title_li='); ?>
    </ul>
    <h3>Archives</h3>
    <ul>
        <?php wp_get_archives(); ?>
    </ul>
    <h3>Search</h3>
    <?php get_search_form(); ?>
</div><!-- /sidebar -->
```

Save this file and re-load your theme, and you'll see that your dummy text has been replaced with WordPress output for the **Categories** and **Archives** lists, and the **Search** form.

In my case, the search form doesn't look quite the way I want:

So I'm going to add these WordPress styles to my stylesheet to hide the label and the submit button:

```
.hidden, #searchsubmit {
    display: none;
}
```

Main column—the loop

The most important part of the WordPress code comes next. It's called the *loop* and it's an essential part of your theme. The *loop*'s job is to display your posts in chronological order, choosing only those posts which are appropriate. You need to put all of your other post tags inside the *loop*. The basic *loop* text, which has to surround your post information, is displayed using this code:

```
<?php if (have_posts()) : ?>

    <?php while (have_posts()) : the_post(); ?>
        <div class="post">
            <!-- individual post information -->
        </div>
    <?php endwhile; ?>

    <div class="navigation">
        <div class="alignleft">
            <?php next_posts_link('&laquo; Older Entries') ?></div>
        <div class="alignright">
            <?php previous_posts_link('Newer Entries &raquo;') ?></div>
    </div>
<?php else : ?>
    <h2 class="center">Not Found</h2>
    <p class="center">Sorry, but you are looking for something that
        isn't here.</p>
    <?php get_search_form(); ?>
<?php endif; ?>
```

There are three basic parts of the *loop*:

- Individual post information
- Next and previous posts links
- What to do if there are no appropriate posts

Note that you can style your next and previous post links using the navigation class. We already added alignright and alignleft, so we're all set with them. Also, we will reuse the handy get_search_form() function that we used in the sidebar.

We are going to paste the loop we just saw into our `index.php` file in the place where the main column lives. In my case, that's the `div` with `id="copy"`. First, however, let's replace the comment `<!-- individual post information -->` with the dummy text from our HTML build. Now the part of your HTML that describes your main column looks something like this:

```
<div id="copy">
    <?php if (have_posts()) : ?>
        <?php while (have_posts()) : the_post(); ?>
            <div class="post">
                <h2><a href="#">Butternut Squash Soup</a></h2>
                <div class="post-date">November 21st, 2008</div>
                <p>My first paragraph.</p>
                <p>My second paragraph.</p>
                <div class="categories">Posted in:
                    <a href="#">Recipes Found</a></div>
                <div class="tags">Tags:
                    <a href="#">autumn</a>,
                    <a href="#">easy</a>,
                    <a href="#">soups</a>
                </div>
                <div class="comments">
                <a href="#">5 Comments</a></div>
            </div>
        <?php endwhile; ?>
        <div class="navigation">
            <div class="alignleft">
                <?php next_posts_link('&laquo; Older Entries') ?>
            </div>
            <div class="alignright">
            <?php previous_posts_link('Newer Entries &raquo;') ?>
            </div>
        </div>
    <?php else : ?>
        <h2 class="center">Not Found</h2>
        <p class="center">Sorry, but you are looking for
            something that isn't here.</p>
        <?php get_search_form(); ?>
    <?php endif; ?>
</div><!-- /copy -->
```

Now that we've got the basic *loop* in the theme, we can replace our dummy text with more WordPress tags.

The post title and the URL that links to the post can be replaced with these two WordPress tags:

```
<?php the_permalink() ?>
<?php the_title(); ?>
```

The date of the post is expressed by this tag:

```
<?php the_time('F jS, Y') ?>
```

The funny-looking code, F jS, Y, is PHP date formatting code.

Learning more

You can look up for more options on how to display the date on a PHP website: http://us3.php.net/manual/en/function.date.php.

Now replace your dummy placeholder text for the actual content of the post with this code:

```
<?php the_content(); ?>
```

Your categories and tags lists get expressed by the following two tags:

```
<?php the_category(', ') ?>
<?php the_tags(); ?>
```

By default, the the_category() function spits out your categories in a linked list. Because I want them to display categories separated by comments, I have to add the ', ' argument that tells the function to put something else. In this case, it is a comma and a space between category names.

Finally, you can set up your comments link with this tag:

```
<?php comments_popup_link('No Comments &#187;',
                          '1 Comment &#187;',
                          '% Comments &#187;'); ?>
```

Here, you can see that there are three options separated by commas:

1. The first option tells WordPress the text that it has to display when there are no comments.

2. The second option tells WordPress the text that it has to display when there is just one comment.

3. The third option tells WordPress text that it has to display for more than one comment. The percent symbol (%) gets replaced with the actual number of existing comments.

The section of your HTML that contains your main *loop* now looks something like this:

```
<div id="copy">

    <?php if (have_posts()) : ?>

    <?php while (have_posts()) : the_post(); ?>
        <div class="post">
            <h2>
                <a href="<?php the_permalink() ?>">
                    <?php the_title(); ?></a>
            </h2>
            <div class="post-date">
                <?php the_time('F jS, Y') ?></div>

            <?php the_content(); ?>

            <div class="categories">Posted in:
                <?php the_category(', ') ?>
            </div>
            <div class="tags">Tags:
                <?php the_tags(); ?>
            </div>
            <div class="comments">
             <?php comments_popup_link('No Comments &#187;',
                                    '1 Comment &#187;',
                                    '% Comments &#187;'); ?>
            </div>
        </div>
    <?php endwhile; ?>

    <div class="navigation">
        <div class="alignleft">
            <?php next_posts_link('&laquo; Older Entries') ?>
        </div>
        <div class="alignright">
         <?php previous_posts_link('Newer Entries &raquo;') ?>
        </div>
    </div>
    <?php else : ?>
        <h2 class="center">Not Found</h2>
        <p class="center">Sorry, but you are looking for
            something that isn't here.</p>
        <?php get_search_form(); ?>
    <?php endif; ?>

</div><!-- /copy -->
```

Phew! Now save your `index.php` and re-load your website. Your theme is in action!

Creating templates within your theme

You've now got a functional basic template for your theme. It works great on the main blog page and successfully loads content for anything you can click on in your site.

However, we want slightly different templates for other types of content on our site. For example, a single post page needs to have a comments form where visitors can post comments. A single page doesn't need to have date, tags, or categories information, but the category page should show the category name.

Before we can create other templates, we need to break up the main `index.php` file into parts so that these different templates can share the common elements. I've mentioned many times the importance of the header, sidebar, and footer. We're going to break them up now. First, let's take a quick look at how it works.

Understanding the WordPress theme

The WordPress theme is actually composed of a number of template files. This allows the different parts of the site (such as frontend, blog archive, page, single post, search results, and so on) to have different purposes. Breaking the `index.php` file into template files allows us to not only share some common parts of the design, but also have different code in the different parts.

As I mentioned earlier, we'll soon be breaking up the four main pieces of the design (header, sidebar, main column, and footer) so that WordPress can make a good use of them. That's because while the header and footer are probably shared by all pages, the content in the main column will be different. Also, you may want the sidebar on some pages, but not on others.

We'll first create these template files, and then move on to other, more optional template files.

Breaking it up

We're going to break up the `index.php` file into these four files:

- `index.php`
- `header.php`
- `footer.php`
- `sidebar.php`

header.php

First, cut out the entire top of your `index.php` file. This means cutting the `doctype` declaration, the `<head>`, any miscellaneous opening tags, and the header `div`. In my case, I'm cutting out all the way from this, the first few lines:

```
<!DOCTYPE html PUBLIC "-//W3C//DTD XHTML 1.0 Transitional//EN"
"http://www.w3.org/TR/xhtml1/DTD/xhtml1-transitional.dtd">
<html xmlns="http://www.w3.org/1999/xhtml">
<head>
```

... through and including these lines:

```
</div><!-- /header -->
<div id="content">
```

Then, paste this text into a new file called `header.php` that you create within your `theme` folder.

Now at the very top of the `index.php` file (that is, where you just cut the header text from) write in this line of WordPress PHP code:

```
<?php get_header(); ?>
```

This is a WordPress function that includes the `header.php` file you just created. If you save everything and re-load your website now, nothing should change. If something changes, then you've made a mistake.

footer.php

Next, we will create the footer file. To create this, first cut out all of the text at the very bottom of the `index.php` file, from the `footer div`, and all the way through the `</html>` tag. In my case, this is the entire text I cut:

```
<div style="clear: both"> </div>
</div><!-- /content -->

<div id="footer">
<a href="<?php echo get_option('home'); ?>/">
    <?php bloginfo('name'); ?></a> is powered by wordpress
</div><!-- /footer -->
</div><!-- /container -->

</body>
</html>
```

Paste the text you just cut into a new `footer.php` file that you create within your `theme` folder.

Now at the very bottom of the `index.php` file (where you just cut the footer text from) write in this line of WordPress PHP code:

```
<?php get_footer(); ?>
```

This is a special WordPress function that includes the `footer.php` file you just created. Again, you should save everything and re-load your website to make sure nothing changes.

sidebar.php

There is just one more essential template file to create. For this one, cut out the entire `div` containing your sidebar. In my case, it's this text:

```
<div id="sidebar">
    <h3 class="first">Categories</h3>
    <ul>
        <?php wp_list_categories('title_li='); ?>
    </ul>
    <h3>Archives</h3>
    <ul>
        <?php wp_get_archives(); ?>
    </ul>
    <h3>Search</h3>
    <?php get_search_form(); ?>
</div><!-- /sidebar -->
```

Paste this text into a new file in your `theme` folder called `sidebar.php`.

Now in `index.php`, add this function in the place you just cut your sidebar from:

```
<?php get_sidebar(); ?>
```

This will include the sidebar. In the case of my design, I will want the sidebar on every page. So it's not very crucial for it to be a separate file. I could have included it in the `footer.php` file. But in some templates, including the default template that came with your WordPress installation, the designer prefers to not include the sidebar in some views such as the **Page** and single posts.

Your four template files

You've now got four template files in your `theme` folder: `header.php`, `footer.php`, `sidebar.php`, and the now-much-shorter `index.php`. By the way, my `index.php` file now has only the three WordPress functions and the *loop*. This is the entire file:

```
<?php get_header(); ?>
<div id="copy">
    <?php if (have_posts()) : ?>
        <?php while (have_posts()) : the_post(); ?>
            <div class="post">
                <h2><a href="<?php the_permalink() ?>">
                    <?php the_title(); ?></a></h2>
                <div class="post-date"><?php the_time('F jS, Y') ?></div>
                <?php the_content(); ?>
```

```
          <div class="categories">Posted in:
             <?php the_category(', ') ?></div>
          <div class="tags">Tags: <?php the_tags(); ?></div>
          <div class="comments">
             <?php comments_popup_link('No Comments &#187;',
                                       '1 Comment &#187;',
                                       '% Comments &#187;'); ?>
          </div>
       </div>
    <?php endwhile; ?>

    <div class="navigation">
       <div class="alignleft">
          <?php next_posts_link('&laquo; Older Entries') ?></div>
       <div class="alignright">
          <?php previous_posts_link('Newer Entries &raquo;') ?>
       </div>
    </div>
 <?php else : ?>
    <h2 class="center">Not Found</h2>
    <p class="center">Sorry, but you are looking for something that
       isn't here.</p>
    <?php get_search_form(); ?>
 <?php endif; ?>
</div><!-- /copy -->

<?php get_sidebar(); ?>

<?php get_footer(); ?>
```

After creating individual template files my theme folder looks like this:

This whole cutting-and-pasting process to create these four files was just to set the scene for the real goal of making alternative template files.

Archive template

WordPress is now using the `index.php` template file for every view on your site. Let's make a new file—one that will be used when viewing a monthly archive, category archive, or tag archive.

To create your archive template, make a copy of `index.php` and name this copy `archive.php`. When someone is viewing a category or a monthly archive of my site, I want them to see an excerpt of the post content instead of the full post content. So, I edit `archive.php` and replace `the_content()` with `the_excerpt()`.

Now navigate to a monthly archive on the site by clicking on one of the month names in the sidebar. This is how it will look now:

Instead of showing the full body of the post, WordPress has printed the first 55 words of the content followed by **[...]**. But if you go back to the main page of the blog, you can see that it still displays the full content. This is the power of template files.

Let's make one more change to the archive template. I'd like it to display a message that lets the users know what type of archive page they are on. To do that, just add this code inside `copy div`:

```
<h2 class="pagetitle">
    <?php if (is_category()) { ?>
    Archive for the '<?php single_cat_title(); ?>' Category
    <?php } elseif( is_tag() ) { ?>
    Posts Tagged '<?php single_tag_title(); ?>'
    <?php } elseif (is_month()) { ?>
    Archive for <?php the_time('F, Y'); ?>
    <?php } ?>
</h2>
```

I also added a new style to my stylesheet to color this class dark grey.

Now when I click on a month, category, or tag, I see a new heading at the top of the page that lets me know where I am:

Single template

The next template we need to create is for the single post view. To view a single post, you can usually just click on the post title. Right now, the single post page looks like the site's front page (because it's using `index.php`); except with just one post. At the very least, this page should have a comment form added!

To get started, again make a copy of `index.php` and name the copy `single.php`. This is the template that WordPress will look for first when it's serving a single post. If it doesn't find `single.php`, it'll use `index.php`.

To add a comment form to `single.php`, simply add the following code just before `<?php endwhile; ?>`:

```
<?php comments_template(); ?>
```

Now when you view an individual post, you'll see that the comment form has appeared.

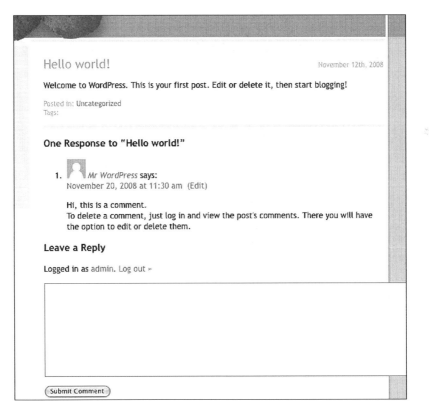

WordPress prints the `<textarea>` tag with `width="100%"`, so you may want to add something like this to your stylesheet:

```
#copy textarea {
    width: 550px;
}
```

There are two other changes I recommend for `single.php`:

1. Remove the code for next posts and previous posts.

2. Add code to display links for next post and previous post.

To remove the code for the previous and next posts, which is only relevant on pages that show multiple posts at a time, just delete the entire `div` with `class="navigation"`:

```
<div class="navigation">
    <div class="alignleft">
        <?php next_posts_link('&laquo; Older Entries') ?></div>
    <div class="alignright">
        <?php previous_posts_link('Newer Entries &raquo;') ?></div>
</div>
```

To add links to the next and previous single post, insert this code near the top of the page just above `class="post" div`:

```
<div class="navigation">
    <div class="alignleft">
        <?php previous_post_link('&laquo; %link') ?></div>
    <div class="alignright">
        <?php next_post_link('%link &raquo;') ?></div>
</div>
```

Now your next and previous posts are linked to the current post page by their titles like this:

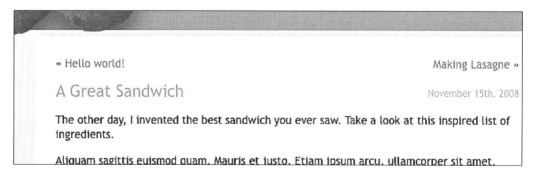

Page template

The last template we're going to create is for the static page view. On my food blog site that would be the **About** page, for example:

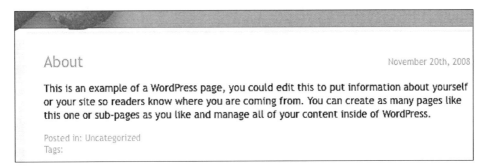

I want to get rid of the date, categories, and tags because they don't apply to my pages. Make a copy of `index.php` and name the copy `page.php`. When you edit the file, remove the code for the date, categories, and tags:

```
<div class="post-date"><?php the_time('F jS, Y') ?></div>
<div class="categories">Posted in: <?php the_category(', ') ?></div>
<div class="tags">Tags: <?php the_tags(); ?></div>
```

As I do not want to let visitors comment on pages, but only posts, I'll remove the comments link as well:

```
<div class="comments">
    <?php comments_popup_link('No Comments &#187;',
                              '1 Comment &#187;',
                              '% Comments &#187;'); ?>
</div>
```

For extra credit, you can remove `div` with `class="post"` (but keep its contents) to remove the grey underline, and then remove the entire `div` with `class="navigation"` because it's not relevant to static pages. Now my **About** page looks much cleaner.

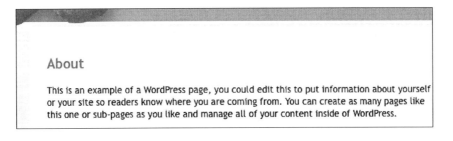

Other WordPress templates

In addition to `archive.php`, `single.php`, and `page.php`, there are a number of other standard template files that WordPress looks for before using `index.php` for particular views. We're not going to create those files here, but you should feel free to experiment on your WordPress installation. These files are:

- `archive.php` trumps `index.php` when a *category, tag, date,* or *author* page is viewed

- `single.php` trumps `index.php` when an *individual post* is viewed

- `page.php` trumps `index.php` when looking at a *static page*

- `search.php` trumps `index.php` when the results from a *search* are viewed

- `404.php` trumps `index.php` when the URI address finds *no existing content.*

- `home.php` trumps `index.php` when the *home* page is viewed

- A custom template page, selected via the WP Admin, trumps `page.php` when that *particular page* is viewed

- `category.php` trumps `archive.php`, which trumps `index.php` when a *category* is viewed

- A custom `category-ID.php` page trumps `category.php` when a *particular category* is viewed

- `tag.php` trumps `archive.php`, which trumps `index.php` when a *tag page* is viewed

- A custom `tag-tagname.php` page trumps `tag.php` when a *particular tag* is viewed

- `author.php` trumps `archive.php` when an *author* page is viewed

- `date.php` trumps `archive.php` when a *date* page is viewed

Learning more

You can find a detailed flow chart of the template hierarchy here: `http://codex.wordpress.org/Template_Hierarchy`.

In this chapter, we've experimented with the uses of quite a number of WordPress template tags. In Chapter 11, I have listed more of the most useful template tags.

Next, we'll explore making custom templates for pages.

Creating and using a custom template

WordPress allows you to create custom templates. These can be used only for pages, and not posts. In Chapter 4 we discussed applying the one custom template called **Archives** that comes with WordPress to one of the pages in the site. Now that we've moved from the default theme to this new custom theme, we no longer have that template. Let's create an archives template for this new theme.

If you click on **Blog Archives** in the page header's main navigation menu, you'll see that it's displaying only the page content:

It really should display a complete list of categories, monthly archives, and tags in use on the site. To do this, we need to create a template. These are the steps we'll take:

1. Create the template file by copying an existing file in the custom theme.

2. Add WordPress functions to the template file.

3. Tell the **Blog Archives** page to use the custom template file instead of page.php.

Let's get started.

1. Create the template file.

   Make a copy of `page.php` within your theme and give it a new name. I like to prepend all of my custom template files with `tmpl_` so that they are sorted separately from all the WordPress template files that I will create. I'll call this file `tmpl_archives.php`.

   In order for WordPress to be able to identify this file as a template file, we need to add a specially styled comment to the top of the page (just as we did with `style.css`). The comment needs to be formatted like this:

   ```php
   <?php
   /*
   Template Name: Blog Archives
   */
   ?>
   ```

   In the WP Admin panel the template will be identified by this template name, so make sure the name signals to you what the template is for.

2. Add WordPress functions.

   Edit your new template file and remove the *loop* entirely. That is, remove it from `<?php if (have_posts()) : ?>` to `<?php endif; ?>`, and everything in between. Instead of the *loop*, we'll add some WordPress functions that will display what we want. Because we are creating a custom template, we can add any of the WordPress functions we discovered earlier in the chapter as well as any other WordPress functions (see Chapter 11).

   First, let's add a complete list of categories and monthly archives. In the spot where the *loop* was present, insert this code:

   ```
   <h3>Categories</h3>
   <ul>
       <?php wp_list_categories('title_li='); ?>
   </ul>

   <h3>Archives</h3>
   <ul>
       <?php wp_get_archives(); ?>
   </ul>
   ```

   This should look familiar—I copied and pasted it directly from `sidebar.php`.

3. Apply the template to a page.

Leave your HTML editor and log in to your WP Admin. You need to edit or create the page in which you want to use this template. In this case, I already created the required page and so I'll edit **Blog Archives**.

On the **Edit Page** page, look for the **Template** menu within the **Attributes** box (at the right, by default).

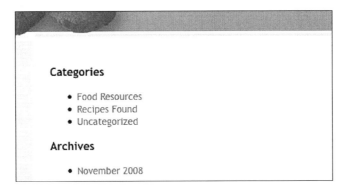

Change it from **Default Template** to **Blog Archives** and click on **Update Page**. (Note that you can also change a page's template using **Quick Edit** on the **Pages | Edit** page). Now when you return to the frontend of your website and re-load the **Blog Archives** page, you'll see that the categories and monthly archives are listed:

Categories

- Food Resources
- Recipes Found
- Uncategorized

Archives

- November 2008

To make this a bit more exciting, let's add one more WordPress function to `tmpl_archives.php`. Underneath the monthly list, add this code:

```
<h3>Tags</h3>
<?php wp_tag_cloud(''); ?>
```

This function prints all of the tags in use on the site, one after the other (inline, not in a list format), and increases the font size of the tags that have been used more often. Save the template file and re-load the **Blog Archives** page to see the tag cloud (not so impressive right now as I have so few posts and tags in use), shown as follows:

There is no limit to the number of custom templates you can make in your WordPress theme.

Making your theme widget-friendly

If you want to be able to use the widgets in your theme, you will need to make your theme widget-friendly (also know as **widgetizing** your theme). Widgetizing is actually pretty easy, and involves just the following three steps:

1. Ensure that your sidebar is one big, unordered list.
2. Add a `functions.php` file with a special function in it.
2. Add conditional code to your sidebar.

Nearly all of the PHP code you need to add in steps 2 and 3 can be pasted from already existing files, so the non-programmers out there shouldn't be too intimidated! Let's get started.

Making sure your sidebar is one big <ul> tag

This is actually not a requirement, but it's becoming the standard for WordPress sidebars among the theme-writing community. As we will be editing the sidebar anyway, let's modify it first to be one big `<ul>` tag. Another standard is that the headings should be `<h2>`s, so I'll make that change as well.

For your sidebar to be one long and unordered list, this means every item in the list will be a header and a list. Once I modify my sidebar.php, it looks like this:

```
<div id="sidebar">
    <ul>
        <li>
            <h2 class="first">Categories</h2>
            <ul>
                <?php wp_list_categories('title_li='); ?>
            </ul>
        </li>
        <li>
            <h2>Archives</h2>
            <ul>
                <?php wp_get_archives(); ?>
            </ul>
        </li>
        <li>
            <h2>Search</h2>
            <?php get_search_form(); ?>
        </li>
    </ul>
</div><!-- /sidebar -->
```

All I did to change my sidebar.php was add a <ul> at the beginning of the sidebar div and a </ul> at the end, and I put each item (categories, archives, and search) into a <li></li> tag.

After making these changes, I also tweaked my stylesheet so that the display isn't affected negatively.

Adding functions.php

Your theme folder now needs a new file named functions.php with the following as its contents:

```
<?php
if ( function_exists('register_sidebar') )
    register_sidebar();
?>
```

If your `sidebar.php` is not in a single big `<ul>`, or your headers are not `<h2>`s, then you're going to need slightly more complicated code in your `functions.php` file. You can look up those details in the WordPress Codex. (Refer to the next *Learning more* section.)

Adding conditional code to sidebar

The third and final step is to add a conditional code to your `sidebar.php`. This code says, "If the person using this theme wants to use widgets, don't show this stuff. If he or she doesn't want to use widgets, do show this stuff." That way, a person not using widgets will see whatever default items you put into the `sidebar.php`.

At the top of the `sidebar.php`, just under the opening `<ul>` tag, add this line of code:

```php
<?php if ( !function_exists('dynamic_sidebar')
        || !dynamic_sidebar() ): ?>
```

And at the bottom of the sidebar, just above the closing `</ul>`, add this line of code:

```php
<?php endif; ?>
```

Adding some widgets

Your theme is ready for widgets! You can now go to WP Admin, navigate to **Appearance | Widgets,** and add widgets. For example, here I added **Recent Posts**:

Be sure to click on **Save Changes** and then return to your website and re-load the page. The default items you had placed in the sidebar have been replaced with widgets, as shown in this screenshot:

Further widgetizing options

What we just covered is the simplest way to widgetize a theme. There are actually a lot of options that you could utilize when adding the code to your sidebar.php and functions.php pages. For example, there are options that allow you to:

- Widgetize more than one sidebar
- Widgetize a part of your sidebar, but leave in some default items
- Widgetize a sidebar that is not one big long <ul>
- Widgetize a sidebar whose item titles are not <h2>s
- Customize the search form widget

Learning more

To learn about the variety of options available and how to take advantage of them, take a look at the Codex: http://codex.wordpress.org/Widgetizing_Themes.

Sharing your theme

If you want to turn your template into a package that other people can use, you just have to take the following steps:

1. Remove all unnecessary files from your theme's folder. Be sure you don't have backup versions or old copies of any of your files. If you do delete any files, be sure to re-test your theme to ensure you didn't accidentally delete something important.

2. Make sure the comment at the top of the `style.css` file is complete and accurate.

3. Create a `Readme.txt` file. This is a good place to let future users know what version of WordPress your theme is compatible with and if it has any special features or requirements.

4. Zip the folder and post your theme ZIP file on your own website for people to download, or post it directly in the WordPress **Theme Directory** at `http://wordpress.org/extend/themes`.

These steps are outlined in a rather general way. If you'd like more details on the process of preparing and sharing your theme in the WordPress community, I highly recommend taking a look at the book *"WordPress Theme Design", Packt Publishing, 9781847193094*. In this book, the author spends an entire chapter discussing the details involved with sharing your theme and makes recommendations regarding licensing, alternative packaging techniques, getting feedback, versioning, and tracking theme usage.

Summary

You have now crossed to the other side of the theming world. You have learned how to make your own theme. With just the most basic HTML and CSS abilities, you can create a design and turn it into a fully functional WordPress theme.

In this chapter we saw how to:

- Turn your HTML build into a basic theme
- Create WordPress templates to influence the display of a variety of views on your site
- Create custom templates to be applied to pages within your site
- Make your new theme widget-ready
- Share your theme with everyone else in the WordPress community

7
Feeds and Podcasting

With so many interesting blogs available on the Internet, many readers find it time-consuming and difficult to remember to visit them all. Even though your blog has a beautiful design, widgets, pages, and photos, many of your users will be most interested in being up-to-date with your content. But will they really bother to remember to visit your site, or to know how often you update it?

Feeds were developed to address this problem. A web feed is a data format that allows a content publisher to syndicate, and consumers to subscribe. With some kinds of feeds, an aggregator can pull in data from a variety of feeds (based on criteria) to create an aggregated feed. (Mozilla Thunderbird, iTunes, Google Reader, and Google News are all examples of aggregators.) Other websites can pull in the data from a feed and display it in another format (for example HTML). This method of distributing information (via feed, rather than via one static web page) is the basic idea behind Web 2.0 (read as "two point oh").

In this chapter, you will learn about feeds, how to provide feeds for your own website's content, how to draw in to your website feeds from other websites, and some useful plugins to make all this happen.

Feed basics

Feeds are short summaries of content presented in a structured way via XML, and are usually organized with the most recent information on top. You can always stay up to date using feed aggregators (software that can read feeds). Using them, you can also have the content you want delivered or collected for you in the way and place you want. This applies not only to written content from blogs or new websites, but also audio and video content (that is, podcasts).

Typically, web feeds are either in **RSS (Really Simple Syndication)** or Atom format. RSS has changed over the past decade, and thus is often referred by a version number. The most up-to-date version of RSS is RSS 2.0.1. The older versions that are still somewhat in use are 0.91 and 1.0. For our purposes in this book, we'll use RSS 2; but you should know that some software is only capable of reading the older versions. If you ever find that you have readers on your blog who write to you complaining that their feed reader can't read your RSS feed, then you could consider publishing links for the older formats (we'll review how to do that later in the chapter), or using a web tool (such as FeedBurner). Tools such as these can serve up feeds in different formats, so your visitors can receive your content in whichever way they choose.

Feed readers

Your subscribers will read your content using a feed reader. **Feed readers** are either web-based or client-side software, which grab the XML content from all the feeds you want and format it legibly. WordPress keeps this in mind and encourages you to format your posts such that they come in through the feed readers.

You may want to take a look at your blog in a few feed readers to see how your content looks.

Bloglines and **Google Reader** are the most popular online feed-reading tools. You can easily add new feeds, organize them into folders and sections, see which feeds have been updated, and also see which items within each feed you have already read.

Feedreader and **Thunderbird** are two easy-to-use and free feed readers. You can download and install them on your computer to control your feed reading at home.

The Firefox browser comes with a built-in feed reader that displays a formatted feed instead of the source XML. While Firefox doesn't provide the organizational or tracking features in real feed readers, it can be useful for quickly checking what your own feed looks like.

Learning more

You can find an extensive list of these and other feed readers on Wikipedia:
`http://en.wikipedia.org/wiki/List_of_feed_aggregators`.

Your built-in WordPress feeds

Happily for you, feed generation is automated in WordPress. The WordPress installation has a feed generator included. The feed generator generates feeds from posts, comments, and even categories. It also generates all versions of RSS and Atom feeds.

You can find the feed generator for your WordPress blog (that we created in the previous chapter) if you point your browser to any of the following URLs (replace `packt:8888` with the URL of your WordPress installation):

- RSS 2—`http://packt:8888/feed/`
- RDF/RSS 1.0 feed—`http://packt:8888/feed/rdf/`
- RSS 0.92 feed—`http://packt:8888/feed/rss/`
- Atom—`http://packt:8888/feed/atom/`
- Comments—`http://packt:8888/comments/feed/`

If you do not have permalinks turned on for your blog, you will need to use the following URLs instead:

- RSS 2—`http://packt:8888/?feed=rss2`
- RDF/RSS 1.0 feed—`http://packt:8888/?feed=rdf`
- RSS 0.92 feed—`http://packt:8888/?feed=rss`
- Atom—`http://packt:8888/?feed=atom`
- Comments—`http://packt:8888/?feed=comments`

This is what I see in Firefox 3 when I browse to the RSS 2 URL:

Adding feed links

WordPress automatically generates even the feeds links that you see above, so you don't have to type them in or remember what they are for. You can use handy built-in WordPress functions to add feeds to your template. Let's add a variety of feeds to our template. We'll add a feed for the whole website, the individual categories, and the comments on posts.

Feeds for the whole website

Let's add feeds for all the posts and comments on the website. If you're not already using the theme we created in Chapter 6, you may want to download it now from `http://www.packtpub.com/files/code/6569_Code.zip` and install it on your blog because that is where I'll be adding the feeds.

Using your FTP software or the built-in WordPress theme editor, edit the
`sidebar.php` file in your `theme` folder. Above the `Search` item, add this code:

```
<li>
    <h2>Subscribe</h2>
    <ul>
        <li><a href="<?php bloginfo('rss2_url'); ?>">All Posts (RSS)
            </a>
        </li>
        <li><a href="<?php bloginfo('comments_rss2_url'); ?>">
            Comments (RSS)
            </a>
        </li>
    </ul>
</li>
```

Now when you re-load your site, you'll see links for those two feeds in the sidebar.
See the following screenshot:

WordPress will generate the feed URLs for you based on your site settings so
that you don't have to hardcode them into your template. If you want to add links
for other kinds of feeds, replace `rss2_url` in the earlier mentioned link with
the following:

- For RSS 1.0 — `rdf_url`
- For RSS 0.92 — `rss_url`
- For Atom — `atom_url`

There's another important way to offer full site feeds on your site. When you look at blog websites, you often see the feed icon in the browser's address bar:

You can click on that icon and see a list of feeds offered by the site:

The code for this is inserted in the `<head>` tag of the HTML where you need to have special `<link>` tags that communicate about the site's feeds to the browser. We have included them in the previous chapter. They look like this:

```
<link rel="alternate"
      type="application/rss+xml"
      title="<?php bloginfo('name'); ?> RSS Feed"
      href="<?php bloginfo('rss2_url'); ?>" />
<link rel="alternate"
      type="application/atom+xml"
      title="<?php bloginfo('name'); ?> Atom Feed"
      href="<?php bloginfo('atom_url'); ?>" />
```

Again, if you have a reason to make other types of feeds available, just add new lines with the options I offered above and replace `rss2_url`, `atom_url`, and so on.

Feeds for categories

Sometimes, a visitor may only be interested in subscribing to posts in a particular category rather than the whole site. WordPress allows you to easily add category-specific feeds.

Using your FTP software or the built-in WordPress theme editor, edit the `archive.php` file in your `theme` folder. (Remember that this is the proprietary template file that WordPress uses for the category page). Add the following code just before `<?php if (have_posts()) : ?>`:

- If you're using permalinks, your category feed code will be this:

```php
<?php if (is_category()) { ?>
    <p><a href="<?php echo get_category_link($cat);?>feed">
        Subscribe to '<?php single_cat_title(); ?>' posts
    </a></p>
<?php } ?>
```

- If you're not using permalinks, your category feed code will be this:

```php
<?php if (is_category()) { ?>
    <p><a href="<?php echo get_category_link($cat);?>&feed=rss">
        Subscribe to '<?php single_cat_title(); ?>' posts
    </a></p>
<?php } ?>
```

I am using permalinks, and so I added the code in the first item above. Now, here is one of my category pages with the feed link I just added:

Feeds for post comments

On the individual posts page, we can add a feed to allow users to subscribe to the comments on a particular post. Sometimes a single post on a blog can draw a lot of attention, with dozens or hundreds of people adding comments. People who comment, and even those who don't comment, may be interested in following the thread, or subscribing to it.

Using your FTP software or the built-in WordPress theme editor, edit the `single.php` file in your `theme` folder. If you're using the theme we built during Chapter 6, find the code that we added in it, which includes the comments template `<?php comments_template(); ?>` and add this code just before it:

```php
<p><?php comments_rss_link('Subscribe to these comments'); ?></p>
```

(If you are not using the theme we built in Chapter 6, you can add the above text anywhere in `single.php` so long as it is inside the `if` and `while` loops of the *loop*.) Now when you look at a single post page, you'll see the subscription link just above the comments form:

Tracking subscribers with FeedBurner

Many blog producers want to know how many people are subscribing to their blog. Unlike visitors to your website's pages, your feed users cannot be tracked through normal site-tracking software such as Google Analytics or Site Meter. One great and easy way to track your feed users is using **FeedBurner**.

To use FeedBurner, which is a free service, you will need to divert all of your feed links through FeedBurner instead of sending them directly to people from your WordPress RSS feeds. FeedBurner will then keep a track of the number of subscribers for you and provide you with a dashboard and statistics.

Create FeedBurner account

You'll need to create a FeedBurner account before you can start using it. Just go to `https://www.feedburner.com/fb/a/addfeed?sourceUrl=http://packt:8888` (replace `http://packt:8888` with the URL of your blog) and follow the signup instructions. You'll have the option to choose your FeedBurner URL. For the purpose of our Packt website, I will choose `http://feeds.feedburner.com/aprilsfoodblog`.

Fill in the other information with the username you want to log in with, a password you'll remember, and a working email address. Then click on **Activate Feed**.

FeedSmith plugin

You're going to need the **FeedSmith plugin**. This plugin will tell WordPress that when someone clicks on one of your feed URLs, which are generated by WordPress, redirect them through FeedBurner. You can download the plugin here: `http://feedburner.google.com/fb/static/feedburner_feedsmith_plugin_2.3.zip`.

Upload and activate the plugin as you learned in Chapter 4. Then go to the configuration screen by navigating to **Settings | FeedBurner**. Enter your FeedBurner URL into the appropriate block.

> ## Set Up Your FeedBurner Feed
>
> This plugin makes it easy to redirect 100% of traffic for your feeds to a FeedBurner feed you have created. FeedBurner can then track all of your feed subscriber traffic and usage and apply a variety of features you choose to improve and enhance your original WordPress feed.
>
> To get started, create a FeedBurner feed for April's Food Blog. This feed will handle all traffic for your posts.
>
> Once you have created your FeedBurner feed, enter its address into the field below (http://feeds.feedburner.com/yourfeed):
>
> http://feeds.feedburner.com/aprilsfoodblog
>
> Optional: If you also want to handle your WordPress comments feed using FeedBurner, create a FeedBurner comments feed and then enter its address below:
>
> Save

As you can see, you can add a comments feed if you want to track that as well.

Starting immediately, the feed URLs that WordPress generates (though they look the same) will actually redirect the user to FeedBurner so that it can collect stats.

You won't be able to see your user data right away. FeedBurner will take a few days to collect statistics on your subscribers. Once it has enough data, you'll be able to log in and see how many subscribers you have, which feed readers they are using, and a lot of other data.

Aggregating feeds

In this section, we will see how we can get and display information from feeds, which are located at remote sources into a WordPress blog. When you display feeds from another source on your blog, you'll want to do one of two things:

- You may want to display it in the sidebar of your theme, with a title and a link for each item in the feed
- You may want to display the title, the link, and a short description in your posts or pages

We will discuss both these ways of displaying feeds.

Displaying an external feed in the sidebar

Feeds come in an XML format. So if you want to fetch feed contents from a remote source, you will have to fetch an XML document. This document needs to be parsed so that the data can be extracted and then displayed as you would like it. In this case, let's use a plugin to take care of all of this for us.

A very simple and easy-to-use plugin is called **Import RSS**. All you have to do is download and install it, and then add the PHP function it provides to your theme.

You can download this plugin from this page: `http://wordpress.org/extend/plugins/rss-import`. Once you've uploaded and activated it, you can add this piece of code to your theme. I'm going to add it to the sidebar, underneath the function for search. First we'll look at the code, and then explain the options. Here is the code:

```
<?php RSSImport(4,
                "http://feeds.feedburner.com/ethicurean",
                false,
                false); ?>
```

There are four arguments that can be passed to the `RSSImport()` function. Here they are, in order:

- How many items from the feed to display (I chose 4)
- The feed URL (I chose the Ethicurean's blog feed)
- `true` displays the description, and `false` displays only the linked title and timestamp
- `true` cuts the length of the title to 30 characters, and `false` shows the whole title.

When I add this code to my `sidebar.php` file in my `theme` folder, I'm also going to give this item a class and add some code to my stylesheet so that it is displayed the way I want.

I added this to `sidebar.php`:

```
<li class="ethicurian">
   <h2>Ethicurean News</h2>
   <?php RSSImport(4,
                "http://feeds.feedburner.com/ethicurean",
                false,
                false); ?>
</li>
```

And I added this to my stylesheet:

```
/* For plugin: RSSImport */
#sidebar ul li.ethicurian h2 {
    margin-top: 30px;
}

#sidebar ul li.ethicurian ul li {
    font-size: 10px;
    line-height: 10px;
    margin-bottom: 10px;
}

#sidebar ul li.ethicurian small {
    color: #666;
}
```

Now when I re-load the page, I'll see the feed items displayed as follows:

Users can click on the titles to be taken to that post's page on Ethicurean's website.

Displaying an external feed in a page

There are a number of reasons why you might want to grab an external feed and display it in a page. You may want to grab a feed from your Flickr, Goodreads, Twitter, or other social networking accounts. If you're creating a site for a department within a university, or a small company that's owned by another company, you may want to display a feed on the home page with news from the parent company's or university's website.

As an example here, we'll display a feed of Flickr images from a food photography community using the flickrRSS plugin.

1. Getting the flickrRSS plugin.

    Download the **flickr RSS** plugin from `http://wordpress.org/extend/plugins/flickr-rss/`. Once you've uploaded and activated it, you'll need to configure it. Navigate to **Settings | flickrRSS**. You can use the handy **Find your id** link to find the ID that belongs to the username, group, or community whose RSS feed you want to use. Here, I'm going to display **20 group** images.

    There are other settings on the page as well if you want to display only a particular set for this user, or only particular tags within this user, group, or community.

    Further, if you enter anything into the HTML wrapper area (for example list item (`<li>`), span (`<span>`), div (`<div>`)), you can style the way the images are displayed.

    Click on the **Save Settings** button.

2. Creating a Custom Template.

    In the last chapter, we created a custom template for the blog archives page. Now we need to create a custom template for the Flickr feed. In your `theme` folder, copy `page.php` and name the copy `tmpl_flickrphotos.php`.

    Unlike the archives page, which did not show any content from the page itself, let's give this page the ability to show page content before the Flickr photos. This means we won't delete the *loop* like we did for the blog archives page. Instead, all you have to do is add the `get_flickrRSS()` function. Let's add it after the `endwhile` and before the `else`. That snippet of code now looks like this:

    ```php
    <?php endwhile; ?>

    <?php get_flickrRSS(); ?>
    <?php else : ?>
    ```

Also, be sure to add the special template comment at the top of the page so that WordPress recognizes this file as a custom template:

```php
<?php
/*
Template Name: Flickr Photos
*/
?>
```

Save your file and return to the WP Admin.

3. Creating the page.

Now we have to create a page that uses the custom template we just made, and displays the feed. I'm going to call it **More Food Photos**. In the content, I'll put some introductory text and make sure to select **Flickr Photos** from the **Template** pull-down menu here:

Now just **Publish** the page and you can see the results if you go to your site and click on the new **More Food Photos** link in the header's main navigation:

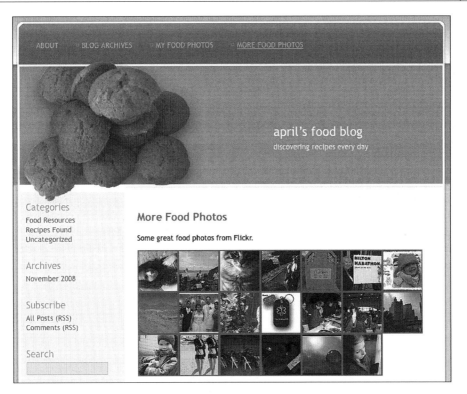

Many other social networking sites have special WordPress plugins. For the rest, you can just grab your RSS feed and use a generic plugin such as FeedWordPress.

Other useful plugins for syndication

There are dozens of other popular plugins for syndication in WordPress. Some help to fetch the feed contents from remote sources and display them in a more stylish way. Some others collect the latest posts from remote sources and display them, thus turning your blog into a planet.

If you are involved with different developer communities, then you must be already familiar with planets.

 A **planet** is a kind of news aggregator that collects content from different blogs having the same interest.

Usually, these planet applications collect news from RSS feeds of very popular and renowned blogs, and display their contents in a single page. So if you browse a planet, you will instantly know what is hot and happening in the community. These are some popular planets:

- Planet-PHP—`http://planet-php.org`
- Planet-MySQL—`http://www.planetmysql.org/`
- Planet-Ruby—`http://planetruby.0x42.net/`
- Planet-PostgreSQL—`http://www.planetpostgresql.org/`

Some other plugins let you do some of these things and more:

- Modify the default feeds WordPress creates for your blog so that you can extend or exclude some information in them
- Display a list of useful links for subscribing to your blog in a variety of feed readers
- Cache feed information

Learning more

You will find a list of the available plugins at the following URL: `http://wordpress.org/extend/plugins/tags/rss`.

Podcasting

If you're reading this book, you probably have at least heard about podcasts. A **podcast** is a special feed that includes an audio file instead of just text, and people use iTunes, Juice, or some other podcasting clients to collect (and listen to) the episodes. If you want to create your own podcast, you can do so easily with WordPress, which has a built-in basic podcast support.

Fun fact
Podcast is a combination of iPod and broadcasting.

Have you ever considered creating your own podcast? It's like having your own radio show and instead of reading your posts at their computers, your subscribers can listen through their headphones at any time.

Adding a podcast to your WordPress blog is outrageously easy. While generating your blog's RSS feeds, WordPress automatically adds an <enclosure> tag (available in RSS 2.0) if a music file is linked within that post, and this tag is read by podcast clients. Therefore, all you have to do is make a post; WordPress will do the rest for you.

How to podcast?

For basic podcasting, there are just two steps you have to take:

1. Record.
2. Post.

Let's look at these steps in detail.

Record yourself

You can record your voice, a conversation, music, or any other sound you'd like to podcast using any commercial or free software and save it as an MP3 file. You may also find that you need to do some editing afterwards.

Some good free software to consider using are as follows:

- I recommend using Audacity, which is a free, cross-platform sound recorder and editor. You can download Audacity from http://audacity. sourceforge.net/. You may have to do a bit of extra fiddling to get the MP3 part working, so pay attention to the additional instructions at that point. You may also want to use a leveling tool such as the Levelator, which can be found at http://www.conversationsnetwork.org/levelator.

- Another option is a free application that runs on Windows called WavePad. You can download WavePad from http://www.nch.com.au/wavepad/.

- If you are working on Mac and want to use a commercial software, Sound Studio is an excellent choice. You can find it at http://www.apple.com/ downloads/macosx/audio/soundstudio.html.

Make a post

Now that you've created an MP3 file and it's sitting on your computer, you're ready to make a WordPress post that will be the home for the first episode of your podcast.

1. In the WP Admin, click on **New Post** on the top menu. Enter some initial text into your post if you want to provide an explanation of this episode.

2. Next, click on the music icon in the media uploader:

3. When the form fields appear, click on **Browser uploader** or **Select Files** to find your MP3 file. WordPress will upload it and then show you this screen with options:

Add Audio   ×

From Computer   From URL   Media Library

Add media files from your computer

Choose files to upload   **Select Files**

You are using the Flash uploader. Problems? Try the Browser uploader instead.

After a file has been uploaded, you can add titles and descriptions.

	aprilsfood-2008-12-01.mp3 audio/mpeg 2008-12-19 15:52:07
Title	aprilsfood-2008-12-01
Caption	Food Blog – Episode #1
Description	Introduction to the food blog podcast. Discussion of what happens when you cook spinach. Recipe of the week. Listener letters. Holiday sign off.
Link URL	

(None) (File URL) (Post URL)
Enter a link URL or click above for presets.

(Insert into Post) Delete

(Save all changes)

You can enter a caption and description in this area. However, none of it will be used in your default podcast. You can use plugins, which we'll discuss in a few pages, to take advantage of the information you type in here.

4. If the **Link URL** field is empty, click on **File URL** and WordPress will put the URL of the MP3 file you just uploaded in that space.

5. Click on **Insert into Post**.

6. Make any other changes or additions you want to make to your post, publish the post, and you're done.

That's it. Your website's RSS 2.0 feed and its Atom Feed can now be used by podcast clients to pick up your podcast.

You can use your own podcast client (iTunes, in my case) to subscribe right away. In iTunes, I go to **Advanced | Subscribe to podcast** and paste in the RSS URL (`http://packt:8888/feed`). My podcast shows up like this:

	Podcast	Release [▼	Description	
●	▼ April's Food Blog	12/19/08	Discovering recipes every day	ⓘ
●	☑ Food blog episode 1	12/19/08	Introduction to the food blog podcast. Discussion of what ...	ⓘ

Here's how things map out:

WordPress Item	Podcast Item	Example
Blog title	Podcast title	April's Food Blog
Blog description	Podcast description	Discovering recipes every...
Post title	Podcast episode title	Food blog episode 1
Post content	Podcast description	Introduction to the food...

Dedicated podcasting

You may want a separate RSS feed just for your podcasts, which is called **dedicated podcasting**. For this, you need to create a category such as **podcasts**. Whenever you post a podcast episode, be sure to assign it to this category only.

Then, to make a separate RSS feed URL just for this category, create a category-specific feed as we learned to do earlier in this chapter. For example:

- Using permalinks: `http://packt2:8888/category/podcast/feed`
- Not using permalinks: `http://packt2:8888/?feed=rss2&cat=21`

Be sure to use RSS 2.0 as it is the most compatible. Also, to make things easier for iTunes users, you can add an iTunes-specific link. It is the same as your other link, but replace `http://` with `itpc://`. If you want to provide links to subscribe to your podcast, you should add something like this to the sidebar:

```
<li>
    <a href="<?php echo get_option('home'); ?>/category/podcast/feed">
        The Podcast</a>
</li>
<li><a href="itpc://packt:8888/category/podcast/feed">
        iTunes Podcast feed</a>
</li>
```

I've added that code to my `sidebar.php`, inside the existing **Subscribe** list. Now that part of my sidebar looks like this:

Podcasting plugins

We just learned that although you can easily produce a podcast using WordPress's built-in features, you may decide to use podcasting plugins to enhance your podcast. Some of the features that plugins provide are:

- Automatic feed generation
- Preview of what your podcast will look like in iTunes
- Download statistics
- Automatic inclusion of a player within your post on your website
- Support for separate category podcasts

PodPress

The most powerful and popular plugin is **PodPress**. At the time of this writing, PodPress's status is a wee bit murky. This plugin has not been updated since late 2007 and the developer seems to be MIA. Also, officially, PodPress works only in WordPress up to Version 2.3, but many people find it working fine in 2.5+. The verdict is still not out for WordPress 2.7.

Learn more about this plugin and download it from:

- `http://wordpress.org/extend/plugins/podpress/`
- `http://www.mightyseek.com/podpress`

Podcasting

Another good general podcasting plugin is **Podcasting** (a confusing name). It is officially compatible up to the latest version of WordPress and offers many of the same features as PodPress.

Learn more about this plugin and download it from `http://wordpress.org/extend/plugins/podcasting/`.

iPodCatter

If you want to have your podcast listed in the iTunes podcast directory, take a look at **iPodCatter**. It helps users create a valid feed for the iTunes podcast directory and specify the `itunes:duration` and `itunes:explicit` tags on a per-episode basis. You can download this plugin from `http://garrickvanburen.com/wordpress-plugins/wpipodcatter`.

Learning more

To find more podcasting plugins on the WordPress website, you can start from `http://wordpress.org/extend/plugins/tags/podcast`.

Using archive.org to host audio files for free

If you anticipate having a large number of subscribers, or if you plan on producing such a large volume that you'll run out of space on your own server, you can use `archive.org`, which will host your audio files free of cost. If you choose to do this, first upload your file to `archive.org` and make a copy of the URL it gives you for the file.

Now you need to insert it into your WordPress post. However, `archive.org` gives you a URL that actually redirects to the music content behind the scenes. This interferes with WordPress's file-detection process. Tom Raftery proposes a good solution on this blog at `http://www.tomrafteryit.net/wordpress-podcasts-not-showing-up-fixed/`.

To implement the fix, do the following when creating a post:

1. Scroll down to the section named **Custom fields**.

2. Select **enclosure** from the **Name** drop-down menu (if there isn't one already, click on **Enter new** and just type **enclosure** into the **Name** box), paste the URL of your music file in the **Value** box, and finally click on **Add Custom Field**.

That's all you have to do because WordPress takes care of the rest.

Summary

Feeds are an easy and popular way to syndicate content—be it written blog content or audio podcast content. In this chapter, we learned what an RSS feed is and how to make feeds available for our WordPress blog. We also explored how to syndicate a whole blog or just posts within a certain category, and how to create your own podcast with or without the help of plugins.

Although different versions of RSS are available, Version 0.91 is the simplest, whereas Version 2.0 is feature-rich. If you want to deliver binary contents or audio or video files through your RSS, you must deliver the feeds in RSS 2.0 format.

8
Developing Plugins and Widgets

Earlier in this book, you learned how to install plugins. **Plugins** are essentially a way to add to or extend WordPress's built-in functionality. There are thousands of useful plugins available from the online WordPress community, which do all kinds of things. In the earlier chapters we installed plugins that catch spam, allow FeedBurner to track RSS followers, import and display a Flickr photo feed, backup the WordPress database, and display titles and links from a feed in the sidebar. You can also get plugins that manage your podcasts, create a Google XML site map, extend the built-in photo gallery, integrate with social bookmarking sites, track your stats, translate into other languages, and much more.

Sometimes, however, you'll find yourself in a situation where the plugin you need just doesn't exist. Luckily, it's quite easy to write a plugin for WordPress that you can use on your own site and share with the larger community if you want. All you need is some basic PHP knowledge, and you can write any plugin you want.

This chapter is divided into two major parts. In the first part we'll create two plugins in a simple step-by-step process. In the second part we'll create a widget. Widgets are essentially plugins, but have a few additional requirements to properly function as widgets.

Plugins

In this section, we'll create a plugin via a simple step-by-step process. We'll first see what the essential requirements are, then try out the plugin, and then briefly discuss the PHP code.

Plugin code requirements

Just as there were requirements for a theme, there are requirements for a plugin. At the very least, your plugin must have:

- A PHP file with a unique name
- A specially structured comment at the top of the file

That's it. Then, of course, you must have some functions or processing code, but WordPress will recognize any file that meets these two requirements as a plugin.

Basic plugin—adding link icons

As a demonstration, we will create a simple plugin that adds icons to document links within WordPress. For example, in an earlier chapter we added a link to an MP3 file. It looks like this now:

Once this plugin is complete, the link will look like this instead:

To accomplish this, we have to do the following:

1. Provide images of icons that will be used.
2. Have a PHP function that identifies the links to documents and adds a special class to them.
3. Have a PHP function that creates the classes for displaying the icons.
4. Tell WordPress that whenever it prints the content of a post (that is, using the `the_content()` function), it has to run the PHP function.
5. Tell WordPress to include the new styles in the `<head>` tag.

Keep this list in mind as we move forward. Once all these five requirements are met, the plugin will be done.

Let's get started!

Naming and organizing the plugin files

Every plugin should have a unique name so that it does not come into conflict with any other plugins in the WordPress universe. When choosing a name for your plugin and the PHP file, be sure to choose something unique. You may even want to do a Google search for the name you choose in order to be sure that someone else doesn't already have it.

In this case, as my plugin will be composed of multiple files (a PHP file and some image files), I'm going to create a folder to house my plugin. I'll call the plugin **Add Document Type Styles** and the folder name, `ahs_doctypes_styles`, is prefixed with my initials as extra security to keep it unique. The PHP file, `doctypes_styles.php`, will live in this folder.

The folder I created for my plugin now looks like this:

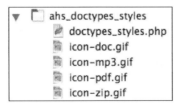

Now that I've the images in my folder, I've taken care of the *first requirement* in the list of requirements my plugin has to meet.

If your plugin has any unusual installation or configuration options, you may also want to include a `readme.txt` file in this folder that explains this. This `readme` file will be useful both as a reminder to you and as an instructional document to others who may use your plugin in the future.

As mentioned earlier, your plugin has to start with a special comment that tells WordPress how to describe the plugin to users on the plugins page. Now that I've got my folder and a blank PHP file created, I'll insert the special comment. It has to be structured like this:

```
/*
Plugin Name: Add Document Type Styles
Plugin URI: http://springthistle.com/wordpress/plugin_doctypes
Description: Detects URLs in your post and page content and applies
style to those that link to documents so as to identify the document
type (supports: pdf, doc, mp3, and zip).
Version: 1.0
Author: April Hodge Silver
Author URI: http://springthistle.com
*/
```

Another good piece of information to have in your plugin is about licensing. Most plugins use the **GPL (GNU General Public License)**. This license essentially means that anyone can use, copy, and enhance your code, but they are not allowed to charge money for it. I've also added a note about the GPL to my plugin's PHP file.

That's all about the introductory code. Now we can add the meat.

Writing the plugin's core functions

The core of any plugin is the unique PHP code that you bring to the table. This is the part of the plugin that makes it what it is. Because this plugin is so simple, it only has a few lines of code in the middle.

The second requirement the plugin has to meet is "Have a PHP function that identifies links to documents and adds a special class to them." The following function does just that. Note that in keeping with my efforts to ensure that my code is unique, I've prefixed both of my functions with `ahs_doctypes_`:

```
function ahs_doctypes_regex($text) {
    $text = ereg_replace(
                    'href=([\'|"][[:alnum:]|[:punct:]]*)
                            \.(pdf|doc|mp3|zip)([\'|"])',
                    'href=\\1.\\2\\3 class="link \\2"',
                    $text);
    return $text;
}
```

When the function is given some `$text`, it will perform a search for any HTML anchor tag linking to a PDF, DOC, MP3, or ZIP file and replace it with a class to that anchor. Then the function returns the altered `$text`.

The third requirement the plugin has to meet is "Have a PHP function that creates classes for displaying the icons." The following function does just that:

```
function ahs_doctypes_styles() {
    echo "<style>\n.link { background-repeat: no-repeat;
                        padding: 2px 0 2px 20px; }";
    echo ".pdf { background-image:
        url('".WP_PLUGIN_URL."/ahs_doctypes_styles/icon-pdf.gif'); }";
    echo ".doc { background-image:
        url('".WP_PLUGIN_URL."/ahs_doctypes_styles/icon-doc.gif'); }";
    echo ".mp3 { background-image:
        url('".WP_PLUGIN_URL."/ahs_doctypes_styles/icon-mp3.gif'); }";
    echo ".zip { background-image:
        url('".WP_PLUGIN_URL."/ahs_doctypes_styles/icon-zip.gif'); }";
    echo "</style>";
}
```

That's it.

Adding hooks to the plugin

We get our code to actually run when it is supposed to by making use of WordPress **hooks**. The way in which plugin hooks work is—at various times while WordPress is running, it checks to see if any plugins have registered functions to run at that time. If there are, the functions are executed. These functions modify the default behavior of WordPress. The WordPress Codex says it best:

> *[…] There are two kinds of hooks:*
>
> 1. **Actions**: *Actions are the hooks that the WordPress core launches at specific points during execution, or when specific events occur. Your plugin can specify that one or more of its PHP functions are executed at these points, using the Action API.*
>
> 2. **Filters**: *Filters are the hooks that WordPress launches to modify text of various types before adding it to the database or sending it to the browser screen. Your plugin can specify that one or more of its PHP functions is executed to modify specific types of text at these times, using the Filter API.*

This means you can tell WordPress to run your plugin's functions at the same time when it runs any of its built-in functions. In our case, we want our plugin's first function, `ahs_doctypes_regex()`, to be run as a filter along with WordPress's `the_content()`. (This is the *fourth requirement* a plugin has to meet.)

Now add the following code to the bottom of the plugin:

```
add_filter('the_content', 'ahs_doctypes_regex');
```

This uses the `add_filter` hook that tells WordPress to register a function called `ahs_doctypes_regex()` when it is running the function called `the_content()`. By the way, if you have more than one function that you want added as a filter to the content, you can add a third argument to the `add_filter()` function. This third argument would be a number from 1-9 and WordPress would run your functions in the order from smallest to largest.

All that's left in our list of requirements that a plugin has to meet is the *fifth requirement*, "Tell WordPress to include the new styles in the <head> tag." Now we need to add a hook using `add_action()` to WordPress's `wp_head()` function, which is included in the <head></head> tag of most WordPress themes.

```
add_action('wp_head', 'ahs_doctypes_styles');
```

Here is the complete plugin the PHP file (minus the license, which I removed for space considerations):

```php
<?php
/*
Plugin Name: Add Document Type Styles
Plugin URI: http://springthistle.com/wordpress/plugin_doctypes
Description: Detects URLs in your post and page content and applies
style to those that link to documents so as to identify the document
type (supports: pdf, doc, mp3, and zip).
Version: 1.0
Author: April Hodge Silver
Author URI: http://springthistle.com
*/

// this function implements the regular expression
function ahs_doctypes_regex($text) {
    $text = ereg_replace(
                        'href=([\'|"][[:alnum:]|[:punct:]]*)
                                \.(pdf|doc|mp3|zip)([\'|"])',
                        'href=\\1.\\2\\3 class="link \\2"',
                        $text);
    return $text;
}
```

```
function ahs_doctypes_styles() {
    echo "<style>\n.link { background-repeat: no-repeat;
                        padding: 2px 0 2px 20px; }";
    echo ".pdf { background-image:
        url('".WP_PLUGIN_URL."/ahs_doctypes_styles/icon-pdf.gif'); }";
    echo ".doc { background-image:
        url('".WP_PLUGIN_URL."/ahs_doctypes_styles/icon-doc.gif'); }";
    echo ".mp3 { background-image:
        url('".WP_PLUGIN_URL."/ahs_doctypes_styles/icon-mp3.gif'); }";
    echo ".zip { background-image:
        url('".WP_PLUGIN_URL."/ahs_doctypes_styles/icon-zip.gif'); }";
    echo "</style>";
}


add_filter('the_content', 'ahs_doctypes_regex');
add_action('wp_head', 'ahs_doctypes_styles');
?>
```

Please make sure that there are no blank spaces before `<?php` and after `?>`. If there are any spaces, the PHP will break, complaining that headers have already been sent.

Make sure you save and close this PHP file. You can now do one of two things:

- Using your FTP client, upload `ahs_doctypes_styles/` to your `wp-content/plugins/` folder

- Zip up your folder into `ahs_doctypes_styles.zip` and use the plugin uploader in the WP Admin to add this plugin to your WordPress installation

Once the plugin is installed, activate it by clicking on the link:

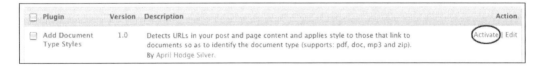

That's all you have to do! Let's take a look at the plugin.

Trying out the plugin

If you look at the podcast post we created in an earlier chapter, you'll notice that an MP3 icon has been added to it.

You can also try adding a new post with links to PDF, ZIP, or DOC files. This can be done by uploading the files and clicking on **Insert into Post**.

When you view this post, you'll see that icons have been automatically added to it by the plugin:

Now that you've learned about a basic plugin that uses hooks to piggyback on the existing WordPress functionality, let's enhance this plugin by giving the user some controls.

Adding an admin page

As you have already seen, some plugins add a page to the WordPress Admin where you or the user can edit plugin options. We've seen this with Akismet, DB Backup, FeedBurner, and flickrRSS. Now let's modify our plugin to give the user some control over which document types are supported.

First, deactivate the plugin we just wrote. We'll make changes to it and then re-activate it.

This is what the new management page will look like when we are done:

These are the steps we'll follow to modify the plugin in order to make this new page possible:

1. Add functions that create an admin page and save the user's input in a new option.

2. Modify the `ahs_doctypes_regex()` and the `ahs_doctypes_styles()` function so that they retrieve and use the user's input.

3. Add hooks for the admin page functions.

Let's get started!

Adding management page functions

The management page that we will create is going to add an option to the WP Admin. This uses the existing space in the WordPress options table in the database, so no database modifications are required. The name of the new option has to be unique. I'm going to call the new option `ahs_supportedtypes` and I'll be sure to use `_supportedtypes_` in all of my function names to ensure that they are unique.

There are six functions we need to add to the plugin so that an admin page can be added to the WP Admin. Let's take a look at the first two.

```
function set_supportedtypes_options() {
    add_option("ahs_supportedtypes","pdf,doc,mp3,zip");
}
function unset_supportedtypes_options () {
    delete_option("ahs_supportedtypes");
}
```

The *first function* adds the new option `ahs_supportedtypes` when the plugin is activated, and also sets the default value. The *second function* removes the new option when the plugin is deactivated.

Let's look at the new *third function*:

```
function modify_menu_for_supportedtypes() {
    add_management_page(
        'Document Types', // Page <title>
        'Document Types', // Menu title
        7,                // What level of user
        __FILE__,         //File to open
        'supportedtypes_options'  //Function to call
        );
}
```

This function adds a new item to the **Tools** menu in the WP Admin using add_management_page(). This takes five arguments: page title, menu link text, the maximum level of user that can access the link, what file to open (none, in this case), and the function to call, supportedtypes_options(), which is the *fourth new function* we are adding.

```
function supportedtypes_options () {
    echo '<div class="wrap"><h2>Supported Document Types</h2>';
    if ($_REQUEST['submit']) {
        update_supportedtypes_options();
    }
    print_supportedtypes_form();
    echo '</div>';
}
```

This function actually displays our new page. It prints a title, checks to see if someone has clicked on the submit button, and if it is clicked the supportedtypes_options() function updates options, and then prints the form.

The new *fifth function* we have to add is responsible for updating options if the submit button has been clicked.

```
function update_supportedtypes_options() {
    $updated = false;
    if ($_REQUEST['ahs_supportedtypes']) {
        update_option('ahs_supportedtypes',
                    $_REQUEST['ahs_supportedtypes']);
        $updated = true;
    }

    if ($updated) {
        echo '<div id="message" class="updated fade">';
        echo '<p>Supported Types successfully updated!</p>';
        echo '</div>';
    } else {
        echo '<div id="message" class="error fade">';
        echo '<p>Unable to update Supported Types!</p>';
        echo '</div>';
    }
}
```

And the last function we need to add, the new *sixth function*, prints the form that users will see.

```
function print_supportedtypes_form () {
    $val_ahs_supportedtypes = stripslashes(
                            get_option('ahs_supportedtypes'));
    echo <<<EOF
<p>Document types supported by the Add Document Types plugin are
listed below.<br />To add a new type to be linked, take the
following steps, in this order:
    <ol>
        <li>1. Upload the icon file for the new doctype to the
         plugin folder<i>wp-content/plugins/ahs_doctypes_styles/
         </i></li>
        <li>2. Add the extention of the new doctype to the list
         below, keeping with the comma-separated format.</li>
    </ol>
</p>

<form method="post">
    <input type="text"
            name="ahs_supportedtypes"
            size="50"
            value="$val_ahs_supportedtypes" />
    <input type="submit"
            name="submit"
            value="Save Changes" />
</form>
EOF;
}
```

Those six functions together will take care of adding a link in the menu, adding the management page for that link, and updating the new option.

Modifying the regex() function

Now that the users are able to edit the list of supported document types by appending the document types they want, we should have a way of telling the regex() function to use the user's list instead of a built-in list. To do that, we need to use get_option('ahs_supportedtypes') in our regex() function. The get_option() will retrieve the value that the user has saved in the new option we just created. Modify your regex() function so that it looks like this:

```
function ahs_doctypes_regex($text) {
    $types = get_option('ahs_supportedtypes');
    $types = ereg_replace(',[:space:]*','|',$types);
    $text = ereg_replace(
```

```
                        'href=([\'|"][[:alnum:]|[:punct:]]*)
                                \.('.$types.')([\'|"])',
                        'href=\\1.\\2\\3 class="link \\2"',
                        $text);
        return $text;
    }
```

We also have to tell the function that prints the styles into the `<head>` tag to use the user's list. Modify the `ahs_doctypes_styles()` function so that it looks like this:

```
function ahs_doctypes_styles() {
    $types = split(",",get_option('ahs_supportedtypes'));
    echo "<style>\n.link { background-repeat: no-repeat;
                        padding: 2px 0 2px 20px; }";
    foreach ($types as $type) {
    echo ".".$type." { background-image:
        url('".WP_PLUGIN_URL."/ahs_doctypes_styles/icon-
                                        ".$type.".gif'); }";
    }
    echo "</style>";
}
```

Adding hooks

We have added our management page functions, but now we have to tell WordPress to use them. To do that, we just need to add these three new hooks:

```
add_action('admin_menu','modify_menu_for_supportedtypes');
register_activation_hook(__FILE__,"set_supportedtypes_options");
register_deactivation_hook(__FILE__,"unset_supportedtypes_options");
```

The first hook tells WordPress to add our link to the menu when it creates the menu with `admin_menu()`. The next two hooks tell WordPress to call the activation and deactivation functions when the plugin is activated or deactivated.

Trying out the plugin

We have added all of the new functions. Now I'll change the version number in my initial comment from `1.0` to `1.1`, change the description, and save the file. Next, I will go to the plugin page and activate the plugin by clicking on **Activate**:

	Plugin	Version	Description	Action
☐	Add Document Type Styles	1.1	Detects URLs in your post and page content and applies style to those that link to documents so as to identify the document type. Includes support for: pdf, doc, mp3 and zip; you can add more! By April Hodge Silver.	Activate Edit

Now when you look at the **Tools** menu, you will see that the new link has been added.

Click on it to see the management page.

> ## *Supported Document Types*
>
> Document types supported by the Add Document Types plugin are listed below.
> To add a new type to be linked, take the following steps, in this order:
>
> 1. Upload the icon file for the new doctype to the plugin folder *wp-content/plugins/ahs_doctypes_styles/*
> 2. Add the extention of the new doctype to the list below, keeping with the comma-separated no-spaces format.
>
> pdf,doc,mp3,zip   Save Changes

If you follow the two steps here on the management page (upload the file icon and add the extension to the option), then that new document type will be supported.

There are already a number of ways in which this plugin could be improved. Some of them are:

- Instead of making the user FTP his or her new icon, the plugin could allow the user to upload the new icon directly via the new management page
- The plugin could display the icons for the supported document types on the management page, so the users can see what they look like
- The plugin could check to make sure that for every document type in the option field there is an existing icon or display an error to the user

Perhaps you'd like to try to make these changes yourself!

A plugin with DB access

There is only one thing that the `doctypes` plugin doesn't do, which is create its own database table. We're going to leave that plugin behind and create a new plugin that makes an active use of the database. Let's create a simple plugin, which stores all the words that visitors search for using the blog's search function.

The database table structure for this plugin will be as follows:

table wp_searchedwords:

Field	Type	Null	Key	Default	Extra
id	int(11)	YES	PRI	NULL	auto_increment
word	Varchar(255)			NULL	

Now let's write the plugin code.

Getting the plugin to talk to the database

The first part of this plugin has to be run only when the plugin is activated. This will be the initialization function, and it has to check to see if the database table exists; and if not, create it.

```
function searchedwords_init($content) {
    if (isset($_GET['activate']) && $_GET['activate'] == 'true') {
        global $wpdb;
        $result = mysql_list_tables(DB_NAME);
        $current_tables = array();
        while ($row = mysql_fetch_row($result)) {
            $current_tables[] = $row[0];
        }
        if (!in_array("wp_searchedwords", $current_tables)) {
            $result = mysql_query(
            "CREATE TABLE `wp_searchedwords` (
                id INT NOT NULL AUTO_INCREMENT PRIMARY KEY,
                word VARCHAR(255)
            )");
        }
    }
    if (!empty($_GET['s'])) {
        $current_searched_words = explode(" ",urldecode($_GET['s']));
        foreach ($current_searched_words as $word) {
            mysql_query("insert into wp_searchedwords values(null,
                    '{$word}')");
        }
    }
}
```

This function also stores the searched word in the database table if a search has just been performed.

Adding management page functions

We now need a familiar-looking function that adds a management page to the admin menu.

```
function modify_menu_for_searchedwords() {
    if (function_exists('add_submenu_page')) {
        add_management_page(
            "Searched Words",
            "Searched Words",
            1,
            __FILE__,
            'searchedwords_page'
        );
    }
}
```

We also need a function that retrieves the information from the database and displays it on the new management page.

```
function searchedwords_page() {
    $result = mysql_query('SELECT COUNT(word) AS occurance, word FROM
            wp_searchedwords GROUP BY word ORDER BY occurance DESC');
    echo '<div class="wrap"><h2>Searched Words</h2>';
    echo '<table class="searchwords">';
    if (mysql_num_rows($result)>0) {
        echo '<tr><th>Search words</th><th># searches</th></tr>';
        while ($row = mysql_fetch_row($result)) {
            echo "<tr><td>{$row[1]}</b></td><td>{$row[0]}</td></tr>";
        }
    } else {
        echo '<tr><td colspan="2">
            <h3>No searches have been preformed yet</h3>
            </td></tr>';
        }
    echo '</table></div>';
}
```

That's it, only two. The last plugin had more functions because data was being captured from the user and saved. Here, that's not necessary.

Adding hooks

Lastly, we just need to add two hooks:

```
add_filter('init', 'searchedwords_init');
add_action("admin_menu","modify_menu_for_searchedwords");
```

The first hook tells WordPress to run the initialization function when the plugin is activated, or when a search is performed. The second hook modifies the admin menu to add a link to the new management page.

Trying out the plugin

As with the last plugin you can now either FTP your plugin file to `wp-content/plugins`, or you can turn it into a ZIP file and add it using the uploader in the WP Admin. You'll then see it in the list and you can **Activate** it:

Plugin	Version	Description	Action
☐ Capture Searched Words	1.1	Captures all words searched on and displays a count for each. By Hasin Hayder, April Hodge Silver.	Activate | Edit

Look at the menu under **Tools** and you'll see a link to the new management page:

When you click on **Searched Words**, you'll see a new page where the plugin is created:

Searched Words

No searches have been preformed yet

The new page shows that no searches have been performed since the plugin was activated. Do a few searches on your site and return to this page:

Searched Words

Search words	# searches
broccoli	6
recipe	4
soup	3
nytimes	1
carrots	1

Learning more

There are hundreds of hooks available in WordPress—way too many to cover in this book. You can learn more about the hooks discussed in this book, as well as learn about all of the other hooks available. Start out at these online reference sites:

- The **Plugin API** contains very thorough information about writing plugins and using hooks:

  http://codex.wordpress.org/Plugin_API

- A complete list of *action* hooks:

  http://codex.wordpress.org/Plugin_API/Action_Reference

- A complete list of *filter* hooks:

  http://codex.wordpress.org/Plugin_API/Filter_Reference

- You may also want to take a step back and look at the general **Plugin Resources** page in the WordPress **Codex**:

  http://codex.wordpress.org/Plugin_Resources

- If you want to submit your plugin to the WordPress repository, you'll have to take steps similar to those you took when preparing a theme. Learn more about the best practices for submitting a plugin to the WordPress community here:

  http://codex.wordpress.org/Plugin_Submission_and_Promotion

Widgets

Writing a widget is the same as writing a plugin, but with a few additional rules added. In this section we will look at the steps to create a widget and you will see how easy it is, especially if you've already mastered plugins.

A widget is just a plugin with special needs

As you read the chapter, you'll notice that there are a lot of similarities between our plugin code and widget code. This is because a widget is a type of plugin. It just has some additional requirements so that it can function properly as a widget.

Top searched words widget

In this section, we will see how to write a widget that displays the top searched words in the sidebar. The user will be able to choose whether or not to show the counts and how many searched words to show. It will look like the following screenshot:

Let's get started!

Naming the widget

Widgets, like plugins, need to have a unique name. Again, I suggest you search the Web for the name you want to use in order to be sure of its uniqueness. Also, you'll notice in the code shown next that I preface all of my functions and variables with a common prefix. This ensures that they are unique as well.

I've given this widget the filename `ahs_searchedwords_widget.php`.

As for the introduction, this comment code is the same as what you use for the plugin. For this widget, the introductory comment is this:

```
/*
Plugin Name: Top Searched Words Widget
Plugin URI: http://springthistle.com//wordpress/plugin_doctypes
Description: Displays the top searched words in a widget in the
sidebar.
Author: April Hodge Silver
Version: 1.0
Author URI: http://springthistle.com/
*/
```

Initializing the widget

Unlike many plugins, all widgets need to have a special initialization function. This is the format:

```
function widget_searchedwords_init() {
    if ( !function_exists('register_sidebar_widget') ||
        !function_exists('register_widget_control') )
    return;
    register_widget_control('Searched Words',
                        'widget_searchedwords_admin');
    register_sidebar_widget('Searched Words',
                        'widget_searchedwords_render');
}
```

For any widget that you write, you can essentially copy this function and just change the name of the widget (in this case, `Searched Words`) and the names of the functions to use (in this case, `widget_searchedwords_admin` and `widget_searchedwords_render`).

The WordPress `register_widget_control()` function tells the WordPress Admin's widget page which function to call when it's time to let the blog administrator choose the control options.

The WordPress `register_sidebar_widget()` function tells WordPress what function to call into the sidebar when it is time to show the widget on the frontend.

Adding the widget's functions

As you saw in the previous section, there are two essential functions that a widget needs to work properly:

- A function that gives the user a control over widget options
- A function that displays the results of the widget on the frontend

I've named the first function `widget_searchedwords_admin()`.

```
function widget_searchedwords_admin() {
   // first check to see if the options have been changed by the
   //user. if so, save them.
   if ($_POST['searchedwords_submit']=='1'){
     $options['searchedwords_title'] = $_POST['searchedwords_title'];
   $options['searchedwords_number'] = $_POST['searchedwords_number'];
      if ($_POST['searchedwords_showcount'] == 1)
$options['searchedwords_showcount'] = 1;
      else $options['searchedwords_showcount'] = 0;
      update_option("widget_searchedwords",$options);
   }
   // retrieve the existing options. if they exist, they will be
   //displayed in the widget control box.
   $options = get_option("widget_searchedwords");
   if (empty($options)) {
      $title = "Top Searched Words";
      $number = 5;
      $showcount = 0;
   } else {
      $title = $options['searchedwords_title'];
      $number = $options['searchedwords_number'];
      $showcount = $options['searchedwords_showcount'];
   }
   // print the items that belong in the widget control box
   echo '<p><label for="searchedwords_title">Title:
            <input class="widefat"
                 id="searchedwords_title"
                 name="searchedwords_title"
                 value="'.$title.'"
                 type="text">
         </label></p>';
   echo '<p><label for="searchedwords_number">
```

```
                        Number of words to show:
                <select id="searchedwords_number"
                        name="searchedwords_number">';
        for ($i=1;$i<=20;$i++) {
            echo '<option value="'.$i.'"';
            if ($i==$number) echo ' selected="selected"';
            echo '>'.$i.'</option>';
        }
        echo '</label></p>';
        echo '<p><label for="searchedwords_showcount">
                <input type="checkbox"
                        id="searchedwords_showcount"
                        name="searchedwords_showcount"
                        value="1"';
                        if ($showcount == 1)
                            echo 'checked="checked"';
                        echo '>
                Show counts
                </label></p>';
        echo "<input type='hidden'
                    name='searchedwords_submit'
                    value='1'>";
    }
```

This function does three basic things:

1. It checks to see if the user changed and saved any options; and if so, saves them. If the user hasn't chosen any options, there's a default.

2. This function retrieves the existing values of the options.

3. It also displays the form fields for the options, displaying the retrieved values therein.

The second essential function is the one that's called when the sidebar (with widgets) is rendered on the frontend. I've named this function widget_searchedwords_render().

```
function widget_searchedwords_render($args) {
    extract($args);
    // retrieve saved options and set defaults if empty
    $options = get_option("widget_searchedwords");
    if (empty($options)) {
        $title = "Top Searched Words";
        $number = 5;
        $showcount = 0;
    } else {
```

```php
    if (!empty($options['searchedwords_title']))
        $title = $options['searchedwords_title'];
    else $title = "Top Searched Words";
    $number = $options['searchedwords_number'];
    $showcount = $options['searchedwords_showcount'];
}
// retrieve word search information from database
global $wpdb;
$result = mysql_query('SELECT COUNT(word) AS occurance, word FROM
wp_searchedwords GROUP BY word ORDER BY occurance DESC LIMIT
'.$number);
$words = array();
if (mysql_num_rows($result)>0) {
    while ($row = mysql_fetch_row($result)) {
        $words[] = array('word'=>$row[1],'count'=>$row[0]);
    }
}

//print the widget for the sidebar
echo $before_widget;
echo $before_title.$title.$after_title;
echo '<ul>';
if (empty($words)) echo '<li>No searches yet.</li>';
else {
    foreach ($words as $info) {
        echo '<li><a href="/?s='.$info['word'].'">
                            '.$info['word'].'</a>';
        if ($showcount==1)
            echo ' <span class="searchedwords_count">
                            '.$info['count'].'</span>';
        echo '</li>';
    }
}
echo '</ul>';
echo $after_widget;
}
```

This function does two basic things:

1. It retrieves the control options for the widget saved by the user

2. It displays the widget.

In the case of this particular widget, there's an additional step in the middle where information on the searched words is retrieved from the database.

When writing the part of the widget that prints for the sidebar, be sure to always use `$before_widget`, `$after_widget`, `$before_title`, and `$after_title`. These are necessary with some themes, and allow theme designers to have more control over the widget's display.

Also note that I've given the count number a span with a unique class. This way, users can style the numbers to be a bit more subtle if they want. For my food blog, I'll also add the following to my stylesheet:

```
.searchedwords_count {
    color: #999;
    font-size: 12px;
}
```

Adding the widget hook

A widget plugin needs just one essential hook. It's the hook that says to WordPress "When you're loading plugins, call this function" and it includes the name of your initialization function. In this case, this is the line of code for the hook:

```
add_action('plugins_loaded', 'widget_searchedwords_init');
```

Trying out the widget

Your widget is ready to go! Save all of your changes and upload your widget to `wp-content/plugins`. When you go to the **Installed Plugins** page, you'll see your widget waiting to be activated:

	Plugin	Version	Description	Action
☐	Top Searched Words Widget	1.0	Displays the top searched words in a widget in the sidebar. By April Hodge Silver.	Activate Edit

Activate it and then navigate to **Appearance | Widgets**. You'll see the widget waiting to be added to a sidebar:

Click on **Add** to add the widget to the sidebar, and then click on **Edit**. You'll see the options slide down, shown as follows:

You can enter a **Title** or leave it blank for the default, choose the **Number of words to show**, and whether or not to **Show counts**. Then click on **Done** and **Save Changes**, as you would with any widget. When you return to the frontend of the site and re-load, your top searched words are displayed in the sidebar as follows:

Learning more

You can browse the following online reference sites to know more about widgets:

- The WordPress **Widgets API** is located here:
  `http://codex.wordpress.org/Plugins/WordPress_Widgets_Api`

- The main widget website, where you can get a lot of new widgets, is here:
  `http://widgets.wordpress.com/`

- Information from the widgets developer, **Automattic**, is here:
  `http://automattic.com/code/widgets/`

Combining the widget and the plugin

In the case of this particular widget, it would be most handy if it were made available along with the plugin itself. That way, people who want to capture searched words only have to install one plugin to get all of the functionality.

Doing this is easy. Take the following four steps:

1. Remove the widget from your sidebar and deactivate both plugins.

2. Copy and paste the three functions and one hook from the widget plugin into the **Capture Searched Words** plugin, and save it. You may also want to change the plugin's version number and description.

3. Delete the widget's plugin PHP file from your `wp-content/plugins` folder.

4. **Activate** your "new" **Capture Searched Words** plugin.

Plugin	Version	Description	Action
Capture Searched Words	1.2	Captures all words searched on and displays a count for each on an admin page. Includes a widget for showing the top searched words in the sidebar. By Hasin Hayder, April Hodge Silver.	Activate Edit

Once these steps are done, you'll see the widget reappear on the **Widgets** page and you can re-add it to the sidebar.

Summary

In this chapter, you learned everything you needed to know about creating the basic plugins and widgets. Now you know how to structure the PHP file, where to put your functions, and how to use hooks. You also learned about adding management pages and adding a widget that is related to a plugin. With your already-existing knowledge of PHP and HTML, you now have tools to get started with writing every plugin and widget your heart may desire.

9
Community Blogging

So far in this book, we've focused on looking at a personal blog, one that belongs to and is used by just one person. However, many blogs are used in a different way—there may be a single blog with a variety of writers, editors, and administrators. This makes the blog more of a community portal or, even more, like an online magazine.

In this chapter, we'll discuss allowing a blog to have multiple authors with differing levels of control over blog administration and content. We'll explore user management for multiple users on one blog, as well as other aspects of blogging as a member of a community.

There is a special version of WordPress called **WordPress MU**, which manages multiple individual blogs (each with just one user) that are kind of "owned by" one master blog (that has mutliple master users); WordPress.com is run by WordPress MU. WordPress MU is not officially maintained with WordPress releases, but recently came out with version 2.7. WordPress MU is a vast topic and is beyond the scope of this book.

Concerns for a multiuser blog

A multiuser blog is useful when a group of people with similar interests want to collaborate and share space to publish writings. If that group wants to publish news on a particular topic, or on many topics in a broad sense, then they'll each need to be able to log in and post their content, update their profile, and so on. For example, I can open up April's Food Blog to multiple users for editing. Each of my authors can add their recipes and discoveries regarding food, which has the potential to make my food blog a richer and more exciting place for visitors.

However, content moderation is also of essential importance to a multiuser blog. The best way to keep a blog clean and on topic is by using a moderation flow that restricts the display of content until it travels through an approval process.

Users roles and abilities

WordPress includes the ability to have an unlimited number of users. Each of the users can be assigned one of the five roles. Let's look at these roles one at a time, starting with the most powerful.

Administrator

When you installed WordPress it created a user for you named **admin**. This, of course, is an **administrator** (and this first user cannot be deleted for obvious reasons). As you have already seen in the earlier chapters, administrators can do everything.

 The administrator's primary purpose is to manage everything about the blog.

It is not recommended to have multiple administrators on a blog. It is best to keep just one administrator for a blog with 10 to 20 authors and editors, or perhaps up to three for a blog with dozens of users.

The examples of actions that only a user with an administrator role can take are:

- Switch blog theme
- Add, edit, activate, or deactivate plugins
- Add, edit, or delete users
- Manage general blog options and settings

Editor

After the administrator, the editor is the most powerful role. This role is for users who need to manage everything about the day-to-day use of a blog, but don't need to be able to change the basic structure or running of the blog itself (that's for administrators).

The editor's primary purpose is to manage all of the content of the blog.

To get an idea of how the screen looks when a user logs in as an editor, let's take a look at the editor's menu (on the right) in comparison with the administrator's menu (on the left):

As you can see, the top section is unchanged. But nearly the entire bottom menu, with **Appearance**, **Plugins**, **Users** (which is replaced by **Profile**), and **Settings**, has disappeared. We can see that the editor is left only with the ability to edit his or her own profile, and to access the **Tools** section, which includes any plugin pages that allow editor-level access (for example, **Document Types**).

The examples of actions that a user with an editor role can take are:

- Moderate comments
- Manage categories and links
- Edit other users' posts

Author

Authors have much less access than editors. Authors can add and edit their own posts, and manage posts made by their subordinates. But they can neither edit posts made by other authors, nor manage comments on posts that don't belong to them.

> The author's primary purpose is to manage his or her own posts.

To get an idea of the experience of a user with an author role, let's take a look at the author's menu (on the right) in comparison with the editor's menu (on the left):

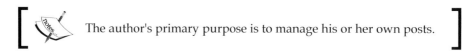

As you can see, the **Links** and **Pages** sections have disappeared, and so has the management page which was available to editors (**Document Types**). The **Tags** and **Categories** sublinks have also disappeared. Additionally, if the author looks at the complete list of posts, he or she will only have the ability to **View**, and not **Edit**, **Quick Edit**, or **Delete**, posts that he or she did not author:

Edit Posts

All (8) | Published (7) | Draft (1)

Bulk Actions ▾	Apply	Show all dates ▾	View all categories ▾	Filter

☐ Post	Author	Categories	Tags
Recipe of the Week: Broccoli Soup View 🖑	admin	Recipe of the Week	broccoli, dairy recipe, soup
Food blog episode 1	admin	Podcast	holiday, Podc

Contributor

Contributors are only able to write posts and submit them for review. These posts will be in the **Pending Review** status until an author, editor, or administrator publishes them. Contributors cannot upload images or other files, cannot view the media library, add categories, and edit comments, or any of the other tasks available to more advanced users.

> The contributor's primary purpose is to submit written posts and make possible additions to the site for review.

Subscriber

Subscribers have no ability to do anything at all. They can log in and edit their profile, that's it. Depending on the permissions set in **Settings | Discussion**, blog visitors may have to sign up as subscribers in order to be able to post comments. Also, there are some plugins that handle sending informational updates to subscribers such as newsletters or email notifications of new posts.

Managing users

To manage users, log in (as an administrator, of course) and navigate to **Users**. You'll see a list of your existing users, which is as follows:

Users

All (1) | Administrator (1)

	Username	Name	E-mail	Role	Posts
☐	admin		april@springthistle.com	Administrator	10
☐	**Username**	**Name**	**E-mail**	**Role**	**Posts**

When we install WordPress, it creates only the **admin** user (which is how you've been logging in all this time). Let's create a new user and assign that user the next most powerful role of editor. To do this, navigate to **Users | Add New**. You'll see the **Add New User** form:

As you can see, only the **Username**, **E-mail** address, and **Password** are required. You can also change the **Role** from the default (**Subscriber**) to one of the other roles. In this case, I'll be selecting **Editor**. So my completed form, before clicking on **Add User**, looks like this:

Add New User

Users cannot currently register themselves, but you can manually create users here.

Username (required)	Editor
First Name	Ruth
Last Name	Editor
E-mail (required)	nobody5@nowhere.com
Website	
Password (twice)	•••••••
	•••••••
Role	Editor ▾

Add User

I can repeat this process to add an author and a subscriber. When I'm done, the **Users** page (where the users can be managed) will look like this:

As with any other management lists in WP Admin, you can roll over a row to see the management links. In this case, you can **Edit | Delete** users. You can use the checkboxes and the **Bulk Actions** menu, or use the filter links to view only users with particular roles. You can change the role of one or more users on this page by checking the box (or boxes) and using the **Change role to...** drop-down menu.

Adding users yourself is not the only way to add users to your WordPress web site. You can also give your users the ability to register themselves. First navigate to **Settings | General** and make sure you've checked **Anyone can register** next to **Membership**:

I strongly recommend leaving **New User Default Role** as **Subscriber**, though **Contributor** could also be fine if the purpose of your blog requires it. However, allowing new users to automatically get any role with more power than that is just asking for trouble.

Next, add a link somewhere on your blog that links users to the login and registration pages. The easiest way to do this is to use the widget called **Meta**, which comes with your WordPress installation. It will add a widget to your sidebar with a few useful links, including **Log in** and **Register**.

Of course, if this is not exactly the collection of links you want, you can create your own widget! Users clicking on **Register** will be taken to the following basic registration page that asks for only **Username** and **E-mail**:

After registering, users will be emailed a password (and the main site administrator will be sent an email notification of the new registration). The users can now log in and edit their profile, or do more if an administrator changes their role.

Learning more

You can learn more about the built-in WordPress roles and capabilities here: `http://codex.wordpress.org/Roles_and_Capabilities`.

Useful plugins

At the time of writing, there were 42 plugins tagged **users** in the WordPress **Plugin Directory**: `http://wordpress.org/extend/plugins/tags/users`. They add functionality that allows you to do the following things among many others:

- Send an email to registered blog users
- Assign multiple authors to a single post
- Generate and display user profiles of registered users
- Restrict which categories different roles of users can use on their posts
- Track which pages your logged-in users are viewing

You can search for plugins and install them on your blog as you like. However, there is a specific plugin I would like to recommend taking a look at if you'll be managing a blog with multiple users. This plugin gives you the ability to edit the capabilities attached to each role, and even the ability to add additional roles and capabilities.

Role Manager

For some reason this plugin is not present in the WordPress **Plugin Directory**. This is unfortunate because it is the only plugin of its kind, and I install it often for the WordPress websites I create for clients. You can download the **Role Manager** plugin from `http://www.im-web-gefunden.de/wordpress-plugins/role-manager/`.

As you can see on this URL page, this plugin has officially been tested only up to Version 2.6.x. However, I've used it on 2.7 with no trouble. After you download and activate this plugin, you'll find four new subpages added under **Users** in the main menu, shown in the following screenshot:

The most useful page here is the new **Users | Roles** page, also known as the **Manage Role** page:

☆ **Administrator|User role** (rename, copy)

⊘ Activate Plugins	⊘ Create Users	⊘ Delete Others Pages	⊘ Delete Others Posts
⊘ Delete Pages	⊘ Delete Plugins	⊘ Delete Posts	⊘ Delete Private Pages
⊘ Delete Private Posts	⊘ Delete Published Pages	⊘ Delete Published Posts	⊘ Delete Users
⊘ Edit Dashboard	⊘ Edit Files	⊘ Edit Others Pages	⊘ Edit Others Php
⊘ Edit Others Posts	⊘ Edit Pages	⊘ Edit Plugins	⊘ Edit Posts
⊘ Edit Private Pages	⊘ Edit Private Posts	⊘ Edit Published Pages	⊘ Edit Published Posts
⊘ Edit Themes	⊘ Edit Users	⊘ Exec Php	⊘ Import
⊘ Install Plugins	⊘ Manage Categories	⊘ Manage Links	⊘ Manage Options
⊘ Manage Roles	⊘ Moderate Comments	⊘ Publish Pages	⊘ Publish Posts
⊘ Read	⊘ Read Private Pages	⊘ Read Private Posts	⊘ Switch Themes
⊘ Unfiltered Html	⊘ Unfiltered Upload	⊘ Update Plugins	⊘ Update Themes
⊘ Upload Files	⊘ *User Level:* 10 ▾		

☆ **Editor|User role** (rename, copy, delete)

⊘ Activate Plugins	⊘ Create Users	⊘ Delete Others Pages	⊘ Delete Others Posts
⊘ Delete Pages	⊘ Delete Plugins	⊘ Delete Posts	⊘ Delete Private Pages
⊘ Delete Private Posts	⊘ Delete Published Pages	⊘ Delete Published Posts	⊘ Delete Users
⊘ Edit Dashboard	⊘ Edit Files	⊘ Edit Others Pages	⊘ Edit Others Php
⊘ Edit Others Posts	⊘ Edit Pages	⊘ Edit Plugins	⊘ Edit Posts
⊘ Edit Private Pages	⊘ Edit Private Posts	⊘ Edit Published Pages	⊘ Edit Published Posts
⊘ Edit Themes	⊘ Edit Users	⊘ Exec Php	⊘ Import
⊘ Install Plugins	⊘ Manage Categories	⊘ Manage Links	⊘ Manage Options
⊘ Manage Roles	⊘ Moderate Comments	⊘ Publish Pages	⊘ Publish Posts
⊘ Read	⊘ Read Private Pages	⊘ Read Private Posts	⊘ Switch Themes
⊘ Unfiltered Html	⊘ Unfiltered Upload	⊘ Update Plugins	⊘ Update Themes
⊘ Upload Files	⊘ *User Level:* 7 ▾		

In the previous screenshot, you can see the capability management for two roles, **Administrator** and **Editor**. As you can see, under each role there is the same list of capabilities. But some of the capabilities of the **Editor** are marked with a red **X** instead of a green checkmark. If you want to add a capability to a role, just click on the red **X** and it'll transform into a green checkmark. For example, I can give **Editor** the ability to **Activate Plugins**.

Now when any editor logs in, he or she will see the **Plugins** option in the main menu and will be able to navigate to that page to activate and deactivate plugins. You can also click on any green checkmark to remove a capability from a role.

If you scroll down to the bottom of this page, you'll find a form that will let you add a new role with any collection of capabilities you choose. It looks like this:

Just choose a name for the new role and check a few boxes. For example, in the previous screenshot I've named my new role **RestrictedAdmin** with only capabilities connected to managing the blog, and with no ability to edit content. After clicking on **Create Role** I can navigate to **Users** and see that the new role I created is available in the **Change role to...** menu:

You'll notice that your new role is not in the filter menu above. That's where you can see that the plugin has not been updated for WordPress 2.7, because this filter menu was introduced only in 2.7.

I can also create a new user with the role **RestrictedAdmin**. When users with this role log in, they will not see menu options related to viewing posts, pages, categories, links, or other content. But they will see only menu options having to do with themes, plugins, users, tools, and settings.

Summary

In this chapter, we learned how to manage a group of users working with a single blog, which is a community of users. Community blogging can play an important role in a user group, or a news website. We also learned how to manage the different levels of privileges for users in a community and how to create custom roles using the Role Manager plugin.

10
WordPress as a CMS

WordPress was originally designed for building blog websites, and most of its long-time and most versatile functionality is perfect for managing the intricate complexities of a blog. However, over the years, it has also acquired all that is necessary to manage the content of a regular website—one that may have no blog, or one that uses some blog concepts in a slightly different capacity.

In this chapter, we will explore WordPress as a **Content Management System (CMS)** for a non-blog website. Starting from scratch, we'll start by discussing the basic design and layout of a site that is focused not on blog content, but on page content as its primary concern.

We'll spend the rest of the chapter exploring how to use WordPress **Posts** to hold content other than blog post content and utilize this different content throughout the website by creating custom template pages in the theme.

By the end of the chapter, you will know how to create a customized website from scratch using WordPress and its built-in tools.

Designing your theme

If you're going to create a customized website that uses WordPress, there's a good chance you'll want to start out with your own custom theme, which is tailored directly to the needs of the particular site you're building.

When designing your non-blog website theme, you'll have priorities that are different from those you had when you were designing a blog theme. You'll still probably want a header with the website's title and also a description (or a subtitle, or a tagline). You'll probably want a prominent page navigation area, which may be horizontal across the top of the site or in a sidebar. You may not need a sidebar at all, or you may want a sidebar that holds child and sibling pages of the active page, or a sidebar with highlighted information and internal advertisements. Keep all of this in mind as you design your theme.

As an example in this chapter, I'll be building a site for an imaginary family farm called **Sunny Mountain Family Farm**. I've had extensive conversations with the imaginary farmers about what they need their site to do and what kind of look and feel they want it to have. This is the design I came up with while working with them:

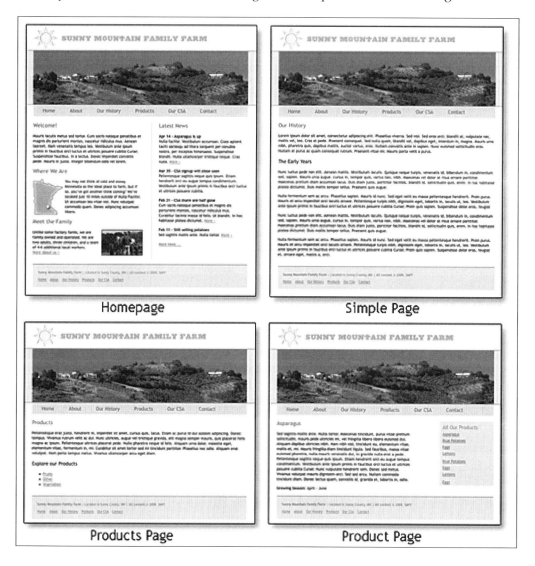

We'll look at each page in more detail as we move forward.

Approach—the flexible WP Post

We've discussed the **Post** in WordPress earlier in the book. It's an object that contains information about a blog post—title, content, categories, timestamp, and so on. When using WordPress as a CMS, we can utilize the WP Post to hold other kinds of information, and not just blog post content.

A WP Post can be a variety of different content-bearing objects, depending on the needs of the site. Each post can actually be a book or magazine article on an event, a pet, etc. It can be anything that needs a title, some text, and maybe a few other pieces of information. By using WordPress thus, it can become a flexible way to manage various types of content.

For the example in this chapter, I'll be using WP Posts as two types of content objects:

- News items
- Product items

These two types of posts will be used differently within the website. To distinguish between them, I'll create two categories; one for each type of item. Also, I'll have three subcategories within the product items category: vegetables, fruits, and other.

Getting ready

Before we launch into the complexities of wrangling WordPress into CMS-readiness, we first have to get initial things set up.

For example, I've been using one blog as an example throughout the previous chapters. I installed the blog in Chapter 2, blogged with it in Chapters 3 and 4, developed a theme for it in Chapter 6, and expanded it in Chapters 7 and 8. For this chapter I'm starting over with a brand-new installation of WordPress, as that is what I expect you're likely to be doing as well. I also disabled commenting for the whole site and turned on permalinks. (Comments can be disabled by navigating to **Settings | Discussion**, deselecting the checkbox labeled **Allow people to post comments on the article**.) This is often the most sensible thing to do on a non-blog website.

Using a simple version of the theme

With the skills you picked up in Chapter 6, you already know the basics of building the theme—from designing it, turning it into sliceable HTML and CSS, and turning it into a simple theme. A simple theme folder will include the `index.php`, `style.css`, and `screenshot.png` files (and probably an `images` folder).

I've turned my Sunny Mountain Farm design into a simple theme. I've installed and activated it before getting started with anything else. I also took the next step of slicing the theme into `header.php`, `footer.php`, and `index.php`. Now I recommend doing this with the re-usable elements of your theme.

If you go to the Packt website at `http://www.packtpub.com/files/code/ 6569_Code.zip`, you can download a copy of the simple version of the theme that I'm using as an example. If you like, you can use it to follow along as we expand on and add to the theme.

Inputting all content

I strongly recommend inputting all of your available content into WordPress before customizing the theme to show everything the way you want, even though that means a little bit of delayed gratification. It's much easier to build and expand on a theme to show content correctly if there is already any content to show, especially because you will need to know some ID numbers for the theme.

This means creating at least a few pages, categories, and posts. (In the code bundle for this chapter, I've included an export file, `sunny-mountain.xml`, so you can use my content to follow along. To import this content, navigate to **Tools | Import**. Click on **WordPress** and then, using the file uploader, upload this XML file. Then click on the **Upload file and import** button. Note that before importing, you may want to delete your default **About** page.)

For the example site for this chapter, I've created six plain static pages.

They show up correctly in the simple theme's menu bar, as in the following screenshot:

After creating the pages, it's important to set up the categories, as explained before. To create categories, navigate to **Posts | Categories**. Here are the carefully structured categories that will help distinguish between product items and news items:

Name	Description	Slug	Posts
News		news	1
Products		products	0
— Fruits		fruits	0
— Other		other	0
— Vegetables		vegetables	0
Name	Description	Slug	Posts

Finally, there has to be some content in the posts. I've created a number of posts in the **News** category and in the **Products** category. Note that every product item post must be assigned to both the **Products** category as well as one of the subcategories.

Edit Posts

All (8) | Published (8)

[_____] (Search Posts)

| Bulk Actions | ▼ | (Apply) | Show all dates | ▼ | View all categories | ▼ | (Filter) |

Post	Author	Categories	Date
☐ **Eggs**	admin	Other, Products	1 min ago Published
☐ **Lemons**	admin	Fruits, Products	1 min ago Published
☐ **Asparagus**	admin	Products, Vegetables	1 min ago Published
☐ **Blue Potatoes**	admin	Products, Vegetables	1 min ago Published
☐ **Asparagus is up**	admin	News	2008/04/14 Published
☐ **CSA signup will close soon**	admin	News	2008/03/30 Published
☐ **CSA share are half gone**	admin	News	2008/02/21 Published
☐ **Still selling potatoes**	admin	News	2008/02/11 Published

Now when I view my site's home page, all of my posts show up listed on the page:

It's time to start modifying the theme to display the content correctly.

Product pages

The first thing we'll do is set up the product pages so that the product items don't look like blog posts. There are three types of product pages. They are:

- Main products page
- Product category page
- Single product page

Main products page template

This is what the main products page needs to look like:

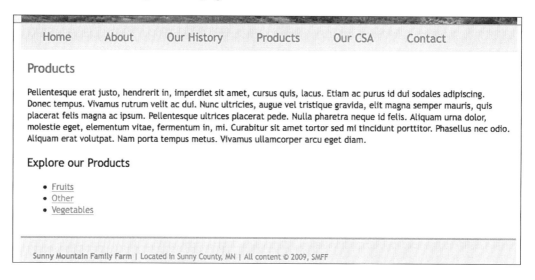

As you can see, the main products page will need a custom template to list the categories. These categories are subcategories of the **Products** category. I could have simply hardcoded the sub-items into the **Products** page, but that wouldn't have made the theme very flexible—if I add new subcategories in the future, they will not show up automatically.

To create this custom template, make a copy of `index.php` and call it `tmpl_products.php`. Be sure to add this special comment at the top of your `tmpl_products.php` file so that WordPress recognizes it as a template:

```php
<?php
/*
Template Name: Product Main Page
*/
?>
<?php get_header() ?>
<div id="copy">
    <?php if (have_posts()) : ?>
        <?php while (have_posts()) : the_post(); ?>
            <h2><?php the_title(); ?></h2>
            <?php the_content(); ?>
        <?php endwhile; ?>
    <?php endif; ?>
</div>
<?php get_footer() ?>
```

Then you can add the WordPress code that will create a linked list of the **Product** categories. (We first encountered this function in Chapter 6.) I've looked up my **Products** category and found that its ID is 3, so my `wp_list_categories()` function looks like this:

```php
<?php wp_list_categories('title_li=&child_of=3'); ?>
```

When I add the above code along with a heading and unordered list tags, my complete template file looks like this:

```php
<?php
/*
Template Name: Product Main Page
*/
?>
<?php get_header() ?>
<div id="copy">
    <?php if (have_posts()) : ?>
        <?php while (have_posts()) : the_post(); ?>
            <h2><?php the_title(); ?></h2>
            <?php the_content(); ?>
        <?php endwhile; ?>
    <?php endif; ?>
    <h3>Explore our Products</h3>
    <ul>
        <?php wp_list_categories('title_li=&child_of=3'); ?>
    </ul>
</div>
<?php get_footer() ?>
```

I have kept the *loop* in the top part of the page so that the farmers can easily write and edit introductory text for the **Products** page. This *loop* will show up the introductory text above the list of subcategories.

The next step is to apply this template to the **Products** page. You can do this easily and quickly via **Quick Edit** on the **Edit Pages** page of your WP Admin.

Now take a look at the **Products** page and you'll see that the list has been added:

| Home | About | Our History | Products | Our CSA | Contact |

Products

Pellentesque erat justo, hendrerit in, imperdiet sit amet, cursus quis, lacus. Etiam ac purus id dui sodales adipiscing. Donec tempus. Vivamus rutrum velit ac dui. Nunc ultricies, augue vel tristique gravida, elit magna semper mauris, quis placerat felis magna ac ipsum. Pellentesque ultrices placerat pede. Nulla pharetra neque id felis. Aliquam urna dolor, molestie eget, elementum vitae, fermentum in, mi. Curabitur sit amet tortor sed mi tincidunt porttitor. Phasellus nec odio. Aliquam erat volutpat. Nam porta tempus metus. Vivamus ullamcorper arcu eget diam.

Explore our Products

- Fruits
- Other
- Vegetables

Sunny Mountain Family Farm | Located in Sunny County, MN | All content © 2009, SMFF

Product category page template

When one of the categories on the main products page is clicked, you see the following page showing the title and complete content of every item in that category:

| Home | About | Our History | Products | Our CSA | Contact |

Asparagus

Sed sagittis mollis ante. Nulla tortor. Maecenas tincidunt, purus vitae pretium sollicitudin, mauris pede ultricies mi, vel fringilla libero libero euismod dui. Aliquam dapibus ultricies nibh. Nam nibh nisi, tincidunt eu, elementum vitae, mollis et, mi. Mauris fringilla diam tincidunt ligula. Sed faucibus, massa vitae euismod pharetra, nulla mauris venenatis dui, in gravida nulla erat a pede. Pellentesque sagittis neque quis ipsum. Etiam hendrerit orci eu augue tempus condimentum. Vestibulum ante ipsum primis in faucibus orci luctus et ultrices posuere cubilia Curae; Nunc vulputate hendrerit sem. Donec sed metus. Vivamus volutpat mauris dignissim orci. Sed sed arcu. Nullam commodo tincidunt diam. Donec lectus quam, convallis id, gravida et, lobortis in, odio.

Blue Potatoes

Pellentesque habitant morbi tristique senectus et netus et malesuada fames ac turpis egestas. Vivamus ac nisi. Integer vitae augue. Suspendisse potenti. Phasellus volutpat aliquet neque. Morbi fermentum. Quisque tortor tortor, viverra ac, placerat nec, mattis ut, nunc. Quisque non tellus. Suspendisse viverra purus et felis. Integer purus nunc, faucibus id,

This page will be too long for visitors to parse. What I really need is a template for the category pages that will list each item by the title, with a link to view the complete information about the listed items. It's time to create another template. However, this time we can use one of the built-in WordPress templates. So make a copy of index.php and name the copy category.php.

In the *loop*, you will see the following two lines:

```
<h2><?php the_title(); ?></h2>
<?php the_content(); ?>
```

Replace the two lines with this new code:

```
<h3>
    <a href="<?php the_permalink(); ?>"><?php the_title(); ?></a>
</h3>
```

A header that prints out the name of the current category would be useful, so add this code before while:

```
<h2>Products &raquo; <?php single_cat_title(); ?></h2>
```

Now the category.php file looks like this:

```
<?php get_header() ?>
<div id="copy">
    <?php if (have_posts()) : ?>
        <h2>Products &raquo; <?php single_cat_title(); ?></h2>
        <?php while (have_posts()) : the_post(); ?>
            <h3><a href="<?php the_permalink(); ?>">
                    <?php the_title(); ?></a>
            </h3>
        <?php endwhile; ?>
    <?php endif; ?>
</div>
<?php get_footer() ?>
```

And when you visit one of the category pages, you'll see a nice linked list of all the products in that category:

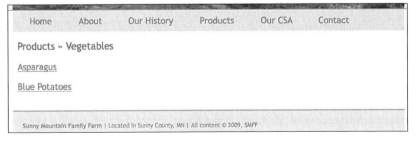

Single product page template

If you click on one of the products listed on a category page, you'll get to the product page (which is currently using `index.php` as its template).

It looks great, but it could be enhanced by a sidebar containing a list of all the available products. Let's create a template for the single product page. Again, we can use one of the built-in WordPress template files. Make a copy of `index.php` and name the copy `single.php`.

There are two HTML tags to be edited. To edit them I need to do two things: reduce the width of `copy div` by adding a class (`narrow`) to it (and to the stylesheet), and add HTML and CSS for `sidebar div`. Once I do this, `single.php` looks like this:

```php
<?php get_header() ?>

<div id="copy" class="narrow">
    <?php if (have_posts()) : ?>

        <?php while (have_posts()) : the_post(); ?>
            <h2><?php the_title(); ?></h2>
            <?php the_content(); ?>
        <?php endwhile; ?>

    <?php endif; ?>
</div>

<div id="sidebar">
    <h3>All Our Products</h3>
    // products list goes here
</div>
<?php get_footer() ?>
```

To add a list of all the products, we'll use a handy WordPress function called `get_posts()`.Essentially, this is the function WordPress uses whenever it has to display posts. It provides data to the `have_posts()` part of *the loop*.

Learning more

`get_posts()` is a powerful function and you can read all about it here: `http://codex.wordpress.org/Template_Tags/get_posts`.

We will now create our own mini *loop* in the sidebar by adding this block of code under `<h3>All Our Products</h3>`:

```
<ul>
    <?php
    global $post;
    $myposts = get_posts('
                numberposts=-1&orderby=title&order=ASC&category=3');
    foreach($myposts as $post) :
    ?>
    <li><a href="<?php the_permalink();
          ?>"><?php the_title(); ?></a></li>
    <?php endforeach; ?>
</ul>
```

The argument given to the `get_posts()` function in this code translates to this:

- `numberposts=-1`: Do not limit the number of posts
- `orderby=title&order=ASC`: Sort the posts alphabetically by title
- `category=3`: Show all posts having the category with ID that equals to 3 (that's the ID of the **Products** category)

Inside the `foreach` loop, you can use many (but not all; more on this later) of the post functions available to you inside the *loop*. In this example, we are only using `the_permalink()` and `the_title()`.

Once you save your changes and re-load a single product page, you'll see that the sidebar has been added:

We'll be using this same function, with a very similar block of code, later when we build the home page.

Adding custom variables to the products

One final thing that is often useful when you want to use WP Posts for some other item (such as products, in this case) is the **custom field**. This will let you add a new data point to posts, so that you're not simply limited to title, content, timestamp, and so on.

For example:

- If you are using posts as articles, you may want each post to have a publication
- If you're using posts as books, you may want each post to have an image filename
- If you're using posts as events, you may want each post to have a location

In this case, I want each product to have a growing season. To add this to my partly built site, I need to take just these two steps:

1. Add a custom field to each of my **Product** posts.
2. Print out the custom field on the single product page.

Let's get started.

Add a custom field to a post

To add a custom field to a post, edit that post, and scroll down to the **Custom Fields** section. If you haven't added a custom field before, it will look like this:

Just type in a name for the custom field (in my case, it's **season**) and the value (in my case, it's **April - June**), which will be different for each post (that is, product). Now click on **Add Custom Field**, and then don't forget to click on **Update Post**. Now you can edit other posts to which you want to add a custom field. You'll see that the name you used before now shows up in a pull-down menu, and you also have the option to add a new field:

Displaying a custom field in the template

To make custom fields show up, you need to use the WordPress function `get_post_meta()`. This function takes three arguments:

- The ID of the post—you can use `$post->ID` for the current post, which you will almost always want to display on your page.
- The name of the custom field—this is the name you chose when you created the custom field. In this case, it's `season`.
- Whether to display or not the value as a string—usually `true`.

> **Learning more**
>
> You can learn more about `get_post_meta()` here:
> `http://codex.wordpress.org/Using_Custom_Fields`.

I'd like the **Growing Season** field for my product posts to show up under the main content on the single product page that uses the `single.php` template. Edit the file and add the following block of code below `the_content()`:

```php
<?php
if ($season = get_post_meta($post->ID, 'season', true) ) {
    echo "<b>Growing Season:</b> ".$season;
}
?>
```

I chose to use an `if` statement because if any of my products do not have a growing season (such as eggs), I want nothing printed. Now, when we look at any of the product pages with the **season** custom field, the value I entered shows up.

The home page

For any non-blog website, the home page serves a very important role. The home page has to perform many functions at once. The users need to know whether they've come to the right place, who owns the website, what they do, whether the website is current, and what the most important things about the entity that owns the site are.

A home page that just has a **Welcome!** header and four paragraphs of text will not accomplish all this. A good home page often has a number of blocks, each of which has a different snippet of information in it. Every snippet will communicate one or more important pieces of information to the users and drive them into the most important parts of the site.

If the website owner has the time and commitment to add news flashes regularly, then a list of the most recent items works well on a home page. This shows that the website is in use, is kept up-to-date, and is well-tended.

Keeping all of this in mind, I worked with the imaginary farmers of **Sunny Mountain Family Farm** to design the following home page:

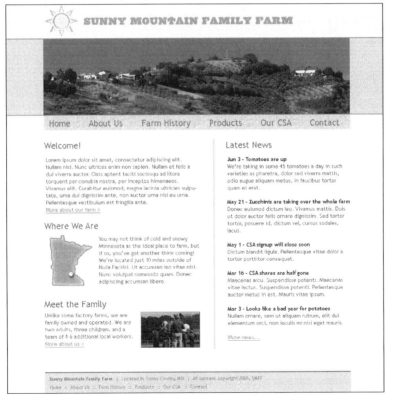

The plan is that the column at the right will show posts in the **news** category. The welcome message will be in the body of the home page in WordPress along with the other two boxes. These boxes will be easily editable by the farmer (who is not a programmer, and wouldn't feel comfortable editing the template directly) via the WP Admin.

Setting up the home page

First we'll need to do something pretty basic—make the home page the home page! Right now, if you go to the root of the site, you still see a list of all the posts on the site. Navigate to **Settings | Reading** to change the display settings. Select the **A static page** radio button and choose **Home** from the **Front page** drop-down list. You can leave the **Posts page** drop-down menu as is.

Reading Settings

Front page displays

Your latest posts

A static page (select below)

Front page: Home

Posts page: – Select –

Then click on **Save Changes**.

Let's also take a minute to set up the home page template. This will be a custom template that includes the existing header and footer, and has all of the structural HTML necessary to create the two columns. We'll add PHP and WordPress function code to the empty space. In this case, the home page template file (which I've named `tmpl_home.php`) just has some HTML, header, footer, and a simplified *loop*. It looks like this:

```php
<?php
/*
Template Name: Home Page
*/
?>
<?php get_header() ?>
<div id="home-left">
      <?php if (have_posts()): while (have_posts()) : the_post(); ?>
      <h2>Welcome!</h2>
      <?php the_content(); ?>
   <?php endwhile; endif; ?>
</div>
```

```
<div id="home-right">
   <h2>Latest News</h2>
   <h3>Date - Title</h3>
   <p>post content for each post</p>
   <h3>Date - Title</h3>
   <p>post content for each post</p>
   <p><a href="#">More news ...</a></p>
</div>
<?php get_footer() ?>
```

Save this file and then do a **Quick Edit** on the home page in your WP Admin to make it use this new template. Save and visit the home page. You'll see this:

Now that the template and HTML structure are ready, it's time to start adding dynamic content.

Inserting the news items

As I mentioned earlier in this chapter, we'll be using the handy `get_posts()` function. Replace the filler news items in your home page template with the following code:

```
<?php
global $post;
$myposts = get_posts('numberposts=6&category=1');
foreach($myposts as $post) :
     setup_postdata($post);
     global $more;
     $more = 0;
?>
   <h3><?php the_time('M j') ?> - <?php the_title(); ?></h3>
   <?php the_content('More &raquo;'); ?>
<?php endforeach; ?>
```

You'll notice that this usage of the `get_posts()` function differs in some significant ways from the way we used it on `single.php`. Let's look at the differences here:

- In `get_posts()`, the arguments limit the number of posts to `6` and limit it to the category with ID that equals to `1`. This is the ID of the news category.

- There are three additional lines of code at the top of the `foreach` loop. The first one (`setup_postdata($post)`) enables us to have access to `the_content()` and all the other post functions that are not made available by default in `get_posts()`. The next two lines (`global $more` and `$more=0`) tell WordPress to pay attention to the `<!--more-->` tag, which is also not enabled by default.

- I've added an argument to `the_content('More &raquo;')`. This is the text WordPress will use to indicate that the post has additional text, which is not displayed.

Another small thing to do is including the URL to the news category, so that users can see a more complete list of news items than the six on the home page. In this case, it's `/category/news/`:

```
<p><a href="/category/news/">More news ...</a></p>
```

Save `tmpl_home.php` and refresh the home page. Now it looks like this:

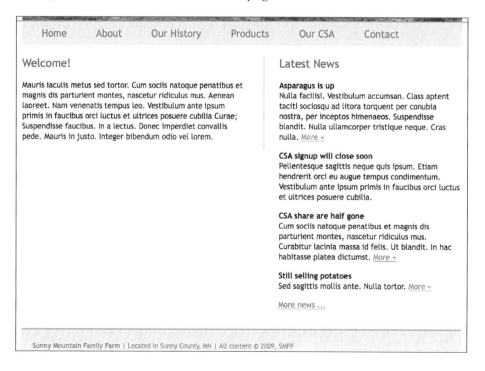

Inserting the two blurbs

As I mentioned earlier, this home page will have two additional boxes with content that the farmer needs to be able to edit easily from within the WP Admin, without having to edit any template files.

There are two ways to do this. I wouldn't recommend one over the other because each may be better suited for different circumstances. Let's look at them both.

Using posts—again!

If your home page design will accommodate it, and if the person updating the website follows instructions well, this is a good option because it utilizes the existing built-in WordPress functionality and includes the latest **Visual** editor. To get the home page set up to use WP Posts for its additional boxes, we'll take the following steps:

1. Create new category and post content.
2. Insert code into the home page template.

Let's get started.

Creating new category and post content

Create a new category that will house some items that are to be displayed on the home page. It's important that they are assigned to a category different from the **Products** and **News** items, so that they do not show up in those lists. I'll call this category **HomeBoxes**. After I created it, I checked on its ID, which is **7**.

Next, create the two posts for the home page and be sure to assign them the **HomeBoxes** category. I often choose to give these home page items the earliest timestamp and even backdate them to a previous year. This will make it easy to find them in the WP Admin because they'll always be at the very end.

I also made note of the IDs of these two posts. They are 55 and 59.

Inserting code into the home page template

For this, you can once again use the `get_posts()` function. You can grab multiple posts' IDs with this one call:

```
$myposts = get_posts('include=55,59');
```

Or, you can call them separately (if you want) to display them in different places, or if you don't want them displayed in timestamp order:

```
$post1 = get_posts('include=55');
$post2 = get_posts('include=59');
```

For the miniature *loop*, you'd use the code that is similar to what we used for the news posts on the home page. In my case, it's:

```
<?php
global $post;
$myposts = get_posts('include=55,59');
foreach($myposts as $post) :
    setup_postdata($post); ?>
  <h2><?php the_title(); ?></h2>
  <?php the_content(); ?>
<?php endforeach; ?>
```

Using the Text Snippets plugin

You may prefer to use the **Text Snippets** plugin instead of using **Posts** if your home page design doesn't accommodate the vagaries of `the_content()`, or the person who will be editing the site is likely to forget to check categories properly, or you want to restrict the permissions of the home page editor to edit any posts. To get the home page set up to use **Text Snippets** for its additional boxes, we'll take the following steps:

1. Install the plugin and enter content for two snippets.
2. Insert code into the home page template.

Let's get started.

Installing the plugin and entering content for two snippets

The **Text Snippet** plugin is provided in the code download for this chapter, which you can download from the Packt website, `http://www.packtpub.com/files/code/6569_Code.zip`. Alternatively, you can download the plugin from `http://springthistle.com/wordpress/plugin_textsnippets`.

After you've installed and activated the plugin, navigate to **Tools | Text Snippets** and enter any text you want in the boxes. For my imaginary farm website, I only need to use the first two.

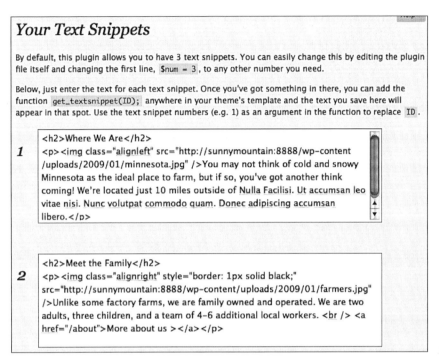

Be sure to click on the **Save Changes** button at the bottom of the page.

Inserting code into the home page template

This snippet plugin comes with an easy-to-use function that simply spits out the text—identified by a number—entered into the plugin boxes. In the case of my farm home page, I just need to spit out the snippets one after the other, so the code I add to tmpl_homepage.php (after the `<?php endwhile; endif; ?>` line) looks like this:

```
<?php get_textsnippet(1);?>
<?php get_textsnippet(2);?>
```

Regardless of the way I inserted the two blurbs, my home page now looks like this:

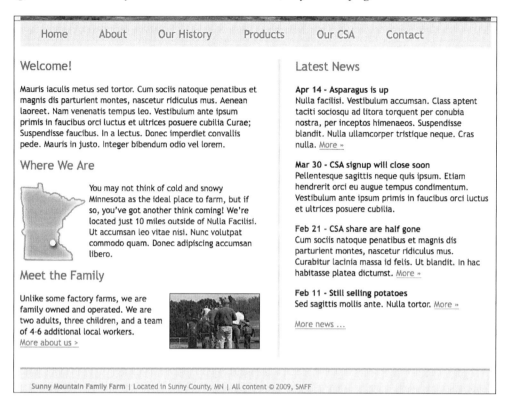

Customizing the news blog

For this example website, we've created two kinds of items using posts: news items and product items. So far, we've customized all of the built-in blog functionality to serve the product items only. This means the category page and the single post page are perfect for the product item posts, but not quite ideal for the news item posts. Our product item posts contain only the product's name and text about the product, along with a sidebar with a product list. The news item posts, on the other hand, should have a date, monthly archives, and so on. Let's make them different.

News category page

I've created a link to the whole news category on the home page so that visitors can view more than just the six items. When you click on **More news...** at the bottom, you'll be taken to the category page for news.

This page can be improved if there is a more accurate page title, some content, and a date for each post. Also, a monthly news archive would be nice.

To customize this page, copy `category.php` and name the copy `category-1.php` because 1 is the ID number for the **news** category. Now you can change the page title, add `the_content()` and `the_time()` for each post, and add a sidebar with a monthly archive as follows:

```php
<?php get_header() ?>

<div id="copy" class="narrow">
    <?php if (have_posts()) : ?>
        <h2><?php single_cat_title(); ?> Archive</h2>
        <?php while (have_posts()) : the_post(); ?>
            <h3><?php the_time('F j') ?> - <a
                                    href="<?php the_permalink(); ?>"
                                    ><?php the_title(); ?></a>
            </h3>
            <?php the_content('Read the rest...'); ?>
        <?php endwhile; ?>
    <?php endif; ?>
</div>

<div id="sidebar">
    <h3>Monthly Archive</h3>
    <ul>
        <?php wp_get_archives('cat=1'); ?>
    </ul>
</div>

<?php get_footer() ?>
```

Note that to create a monthly archive only for a single category, you'll need the **Archives for a category** plugin. You can find it at `http://kwebble.com/blog/2007_08_15/archives_for_a_category`.

Now the news category page looks like this:

Single news item page

If you want to customize the single post page for a news item, you can do so. Rename your existing `single.php` file (which you've already customized for products) to `single-products.php`. Create a new file, `single.php`, which has only the following code:

```php
<?php
if (in_category(1)) {
    include(TEMPLATEPATH . '/single-news.php');
} else {
    include(TEMPLATEPATH . '/single-products.php');
}
?>
```

Now you can copy `single-products.php` into a new file called `single-news.php`. Any single post that is in the **News** category (**ID=1**) will use the `single-news.php` file and all others will use `single-products.php`. This way, you can customize the `single-news.php` file to include the date stamp for the post, to exclude the custom **Growing Season** field, to have the monthly news archive sidebar, and so on. Your `single-news.php` file will now look like this:

```php
<?php get_header() ?>
<div id="copy" class="narrow">
    <?php if (have_posts()) : ?>
        <?php while (have_posts()) : the_post(); ?>
            <h2><?php the_title(); ?></h2>
            <div class="single-date"><?php the_time('F j, Y') ?></div>
            <?php the_content(); ?>
        <?php endwhile; ?>
    <?php endif; ?>
</div>
<div id="sidebar">
    <h3>Monthly Archive</h3>
    <ul>
        <?php wp_get_archives('cat=1'); ?>
    </ul>
</div>
<?php get_footer() ?>
```

(At this point you'll probably want to pull out the sidebar into `sidebar.php` because it's now identical in two templates). A single news item post page now looks like this:

Summary

In this chapter you learned to have ultimate control over a WordPress-driven website that's not even a standard blog. You can leverage the existing WordPress tools to create and manage content that's not blog content.

We also talked about a number of ways in which you can manipulate your custom theme to take advantage of all that WordPress has to offer regarding content display.

11
Administrator's Reference

This chapter will provide information to help you with the WordPress administrative tasks. A few topics that have been covered elsewhere in the book are explained in greater detail here.

I'll review the essentials and then give you some important links that you can visit for more details. This chapter is a kind of a 'cheat sheet' that you can refer to for quick answers to common administrative issues.

System requirements

The minimum system requirement for WordPress is a web server with the following software installed:

- PHP Version 4.3 or greater
- MySQL Version 4.0 or greater

Although Apache and LiteSpeed are highly recommended by the WordPress developers, any server running PHP and MySQL will do.

If you want to be able to use the built-in WordPress permalinks, you must have an Apache web server with `mod_rewrite` enabled. Even if you are on a Windows server, there are ways to achieve the permalinks. You can check the URL `http://www.tutorio.com/tutorial/enable-mod-rewrite-on-apache` to know how to enable `mod_rewrite` on your web server. This is too complicated to be explored in depth in this book, but I encourage you to search the Internet for other people's solutions.

The importance of backing up

You never know when there could be a glitch in your server, or a lightning strike, so it's a good idea to take regular backups of your site. There are a couple of approaches, which I outline in the following sections.

Easy, quick, frequent content backups

The most important part of your site, and also the part that you will never be able to re-create, is the content contained in the database. You should back up your database pretty regularly; although, exactly how often will depend on the number of times you change your content. Here is a rough estimation of how frequently you need to make a backup:

- 20 or more blog posts a week — back up twice a week
- 2 to 5 blog posts a week — back up once a week
- 3 to 4 blog posts a month — back up once a month
- Non-blog website — back up whenever you make text changes or add pages

The question you should ask yourself is, "If my server or host completely fizzles out today, how much time would it take me to re-create what's not already backed up?"

Luckily, your blog content is pretty easy to back up. You can directly export the content of your database using phpMyAdmin or any other database tools provided by your host. Or, even easier, install the **WordPress Database Backup** plugin. It's small, uncomplicated, reliable, and easy to use. You can download it here: `http://wordpress.org/extend/plugins/wp-db-backup/`.

Once it's installed and activated, you can navigate to **Tools | Backup** and download a backup file to your computer. This plugin also allows you to schedule backups daily, weekly, or monthly. It is much easier to automatically schedule a backup to take place once a month or week, even if you update only sporadically. It is a good rule of thumb to have a regularly scheduled backup running no matter how rarely the site is updated.

Backing up everything

In addition to your database, there are other irreplaceable files that make up your WordPress website. These include:

- The theme you are using
- The plugins you've got installed and activated
- The files you've uploaded

WordPress stores all of these things in the same folder called `wp-content/`. Every time you change your theme and install a new plugin, you should make sure that you have a backup of these things on your home computer. After that, you don't need to back these two things up regularly because they won't change.

However, the files you upload are a collection that changes over time as you add more files. If you add a photo with each blog post, then that collection changes as frequently as you post. You should be sure to create a backup of the `wp-content/uploads/` folder pretty regularly, which you can easily do via FTP. If you have an FTP program with a **synchronize** feature, then you won't have to constantly re-download older files, or do a lot of hunting and pecking for new ones.

Verifying your backups

Be sure to verify your backups! Every time you download a database export or use FTP to download files, make sure to take a close look at the downloaded files. Sometimes backups get interrupted or there are glitches in the system. It's better to find that out right in the beginning, rather than when you need to rely on your backups later.

A closer look at upgrading WordPress

In Chapter 2, we briefly discussed upgrading your existing WordPress version to the latest available version. In this section, we will take a closer look at the upgrade process.

 [WordPress 2.7 and above include a built-in upgrade.]

You can use the built-in upgrade to replace steps 4 to 7 in the following list, but you should still carry out the other steps. Also, the built-in upgrade does not work on all servers.

In the following section, we will explain how to upgrade WordPress from an older version to a newer version gradually. If you find yourself in a situation where you have to upgrade across a large span of version numbers, for example from 2.2 to 2.7, I highly recommend doing it in stages. Do the complete upgrade from 2.2 to 2.3.3, then from 2.3.3 to 2.5, and then from 2.5 to 2.7.

You can download the previous stable versions of WordPress from this page: `http://wordpress.org/download/release-archive/`.

The steps involved in upgrading WordPress are as follows:

1. Back up your database.
2. Back up your WordPress files.
3. Deactivate all your plugins.
4. Download and extract WordPress.
5. Delete old files.
6. Upload the new files.
7. Run the WordPress upgrade program.
8. Update permalinks and `.htaccess`.
9. Install updated plugins and themes.

Backing up your database

Before upgrading WordPress, you must always back up the database because it contains all of the textual and structural content for your site. This way, if anything goes horribly wrong with your upgrade, you won't lose everything.

We reviewed how to back up your WordPress website earlier in this chapter, so you can refer back for specific instructions.

Backing up your WordPress files

Remember, the complete content of what creates your site is contained not only in the database, but also in certain files on the server. Always back up all of your files as well, just in case something goes wrong with the upgrade.

Again, refer back to the backup instructions above if you need to review the steps.

Deactivating all your plugins

The plugins that you have installed with your current version of WordPress may not work with the newest version of WordPress. Also, if you leave them active while upgrading, your new WordPress installation may break. So before upgrading WordPress, you must deactivate all the active plugins.

To deactivate plugins, log into your WP Admin and navigate to **Plugins**:

You can deactivate everything at once by clicking on the master checkbox at the top to check all, choosing **Deactivate** from the **Bulk Actions** menu, and clicking on **Apply**.

Downloading and extracting WordPress

Now download the WordPress ZIP file onto your computer from
`http://wordpress.org/download/`.

After downloading WordPress, extract all of the files in a new folder named `wordpress`.

Deleting old files

Now delete all the files and folders of your previous WordPress installation except these:

- `wp-config.php`
- `wp-content/`
- `wp-includes/languages/` (if you have used a specific language pack)
- `.htaccess` (if you have used custom permalinks)

The easiest way to delete the files and folders that you will be replacing is to access your server via FTP.

Uploading the new files

If you're not already connected via FTP, connect now. Select all of the files in the `wordpress` folder on your computer, except for the `wp-content` folder, and upload them to your server.

Running the WordPress upgrade program

WordPress easily takes care of the next step for you: running the upgrade. This script usually takes a look at your database and makes alterations to it, so that it is compatible with the new version of WordPress.

To access it, just point your browser to your WordPress website and you'll be prompted to do the upgrade. Or, you can take a shortcut by going directly to `http://yourwordpresssite.com/wp-admin/upgrade.php`.

Click on the **Upgrade WordPress** link.

Updating permalinks and .htaccess

You may have to update the permalink settings so that they match the previous installation. Your permalink settings dictate what the `.htaccess` file should look like. If WordPress cannot access your `.htaccess` file because of permissions problems, then the permalinks page will display a message letting you know about it. That message will also tell you what text needs to be in the `.htaccess` file, so that you can create or update it yourself.

Installing updated plugins and themes

In your WP Admin visit the plugins page again. If there are new versions of any of your installed but now inactive plugins, there'll be a note telling you so. If you have any plugins that are not part of the WordPress **Plugin Directory**, this is a good time to check the websites for those plugins to see if there's an upgrade available.

You can also take a look at the **Plugin Compatibility** lists on this page: `http://codex.wordpress.org/Plugins/Plugin_Compatibility`.

Once you're sure that the plugins you want to use are up-to-date, activate them one at a time so that there are no problems.

This is also a good time to check for updates for the theme you are using. In the `wp-content` folder on your computer (which you did not upload, remember?) there is an updated version of the default theme, which I always like to have around even if I'm not using it. You can simply replace the entire `wp-content/themes/default` folder with the new one.

You can check for a new version of the theme you are using on the developer's website, or in the WordPress **Theme Directory**.

Migrating or restoring a WordPress site

Sometimes you may find yourself in a situation where you need to move your WordPress website from one server to another. Or, if something gets fried on your server and is restored, you need to re-create your damaged WordPress site. Here you'll essentially need to do the same things as you would in a migration.

The steps for migration are as follows:

1. Download a backup of your database (as described earlier in this chapter, in the section on backing up). This will be an SQL file.

2. Download all of your files (as described earlier in this chapter, in the section on backing up).

3. Look in your downloaded files for `wp-config.php`. Find the lines that define the connection to the database.

```
17    // ** MySQL settings - You can get this info from your web host
18    /** The name of the database for WordPress */
19    define('DB_NAME', 'packt27b3');
20
21    /** MySQL database username */
22    define('DB_USER', 'wordpresssite');
23
24    /** MySQL database password */
25    define('DB_PASSWORD', 'JSTQ89&@j');
26
27    /** MySQL hostname */
28    define('DB_HOST', 'localhost');
29
```

Edit these lines so that they now have the database name, database username, database password, and database hostname for your new database.

4. Open the SQL file that you downloaded in a text editor and do a global search for your old URL to replace it with the new one. Save the changes.

5. Upload all of your files to your new server.

6. Implement your SQL file in your new database.

7. Change the permissions of your `wp-content` folder to `777`, so that you'll be able to upload files without any problem.

8. Change the absolute path of your WordPress folder in the database. You can do this by running a PHP file inside your WordPress `wp-content` folder. The code of this PHP file is `<? echo getcwd() ?>`. Now execute this file using your browser and grab the result. Then run the following SQL command by replacing `/home/user/april/www` with the appropriate path on your own server, on your database:

   ```
   update wp_options set option_value='/home/user/april/www' where
    option_name='fileupload_realpath'
   ```

9. Log in to your new WP Admin and check the permalinks. You may have to reset them if your `.htaccess` didn't come over properly.

You're done!

If you're restoring your site on the same server, with no changes in the location or the database, then you can skip steps 3, 4, and 8. Steps 1 and 2 (to back up) should be done before the meltdown!

Setting file permissions

To install and maintain WordPress properly, you may need to change permissions to different files and folders in the WordPress folder. If you are using a Windows operating system, then file permissions don't matter. If your server is running on Unix, permissions do matter.

What are file permissions?

File permissions are settings that indicate who is privileged to do what. That is, in Linux some users may have the permissions to alter the content of a file, some may have a permit just to read it, or some may not even have read/write access. Besides read/write permissions, there are also "execute" permissions. If a file is executable, then this permission indicates who can execute that file. Before setting permissions for WordPress, let's discuss the significance of the following files and folders:

- `/ or root`: This is the root folder that contains all WordPress files and folders. If your WordPress folder resides in `/home/user/april/www/wp/`, then your root folder for WordPress is the `wp` folder. All the files in this folder must be writable only by you.

- `/wp-admin`: This folder contains all the functions and files required for administering WordPress. This folder must be writable by general users, or at least by users who have privileges to upload plugins or modify themes.

- `/wp-includes`: This is the place where all WordPress core files reside. This folder must be writable by the owner, which means "you."

- `/wp-content`: This is the folder that contains user files such as themes, plugins, uploaded images, and so on. This must be writable by your user account.

- `/wp-content/themes`: This is the folder that contains themes. If you use the custom theme editor that comes with WordPress, you may set this folder to writable.

- `/wp-content/plugins`: This is the folder that contains plugins. This folder may or may not be writable, depending upon the plugins you use.

- `/.htaccess`: If you decide to use custom permalinks, this must be writable by your user account. If you allow custom permalinks or formatted URLs managed automatically by WordPress, then you must give write permission to this file.

For file permissions at a glance, look at the following chart:

File/Folder	Owner Permission	Group Permission	User Permission	Total	Numerical Equivalent
/	rwx	rw	rw	rwxrw-rw-	766
/.htaccess	rwx	rw	rw	rwxrw-rw-	766
/wp-admin	rwx	r--	r--	rwxr--r--	744
/wp-includes	rwx	r--	r--	rwxr--r--	744
/wp-content	rwx	rwx	rw-	rwxrwxrw-	776
/wp-content/ themes	rwx	rwx	rw-	rwxrwxrw-	776
/wp-content/ plugins	rwx	rw-	rw-	rwxrw-rw-	766

How to set permissions

You can change permissions to files and folders using any FTP client. If you have shell access, you can even apply shell commands for changing file permissions. If you're using an FTP client, select the files you want to change permissions for and look for menus like **Get Info**, **File Attributes**, or **Change Permissions**. There will be a GUI, often with checkboxes, that lets you choose permissions for different files.

If you are using shell, change the file permissions with the `chmod` command. For example, the `wp-admin` folder should be set as `rwxr--r--` or `744`; and to change the permissions for the `wp-admin/` folder, run the following command:

```
chmod -R wp-admin 744
```

Troubleshooting

In this section, we will discuss the problems that may arise during the installation and execution of WordPress and provide solutions for troubleshooting them.

Troubleshooting during installation

Most of the problems discussed here have been taken from the WordPress installation **FAQs (Frequently Asked Questions)** and **Troubleshooting FAQs**.

Headers already sent

Problem : Sometimes, when you point your browser to the blog, you may get an error that displays a **headers already sent** message on your page. The whole page may look scrambled and it will not function.

Cause: WordPress uses PHP session functions. If anything is displayed before these session functions, which may even be a blank space, then the session functions will not work properly. This happens because your browser has already received all headers and it starts displaying the output. In such circumstances, this error may occur.

Solution: You have to figure out where the error has occurred. Mostly, it is a file that you have edited manually. If you remember, you edited the `wp-config.php` file while installing WordPress. Open the file with your text editor and make sure that there is nothing before `<?` in the first line and after `?>` in the last line. Now save this file, upload it to your WordPress folder, and refresh your page again.

Page comes with only PHP code

Problem: When you open a PHP page it displays the PHP code instead of its contents.

Cause: This could only happen when your server cannot parse PHP properly. This is a problem of your server configuration; either PHP is not installed on your server or it is not configured to function properly.

Solution: To solve this problem, contact the system administrator for your server or try installing PHP.

Cannot connect to MySQL database

Problem: WordPress cannot connect to the MySQL database, and is displaying an error.

Cause: This might happen if:

- The database parameters are incorrect
- The daemon/service is not running properly
- In MySQL Version 4.1 and later, the password encryption settings have been changed a bit, as a result of which PHP cannot connect to some versions of MySQL

Solution: To solve this problem you can try the following:

1. Open your `wp-config.php` file and check whether the database parameters are correct.
2. If you are sure that these settings are fine, please check if the MySQL daemon/service is running properly. If MySQL is not running, run this service. If MySQL is already running, try restarting the service.
3. If you are sure that your database parameters are fine and MySQL is also running, then connect to MySQL using your MySQL command-line tool and apply these commands:

   ```
   set password = OLD_PASSWORD('your_current_password');
   flush privileges;
   ```

   This will use old encryption of passwords so that PHP can connect to MySQL.

Basic troubleshooting

The best place where you can find help for WordPress is its own help system, `http://codex.wordpress.org/Troubleshooting`. No other site is comparable with it. The following are some basic and common problems that you may face while using WordPress.

Cannot see posts

Problem: Posts are not seen and the message that search doesn't meet criteria is displayed.

Cause: This can happen because of caching. For example, you have searched once and WordPress stored the search result inside its cache; so every time you visit the page you see the old result.

Solution: You can solve this problem by clearing the cache and cookies from your browser. For this problem, you may also check `search.php` and `index.php` for errors.

Making a blog totally private

Need: If you are running your blog for a personal and private group (or for your own official department) so that only members of your group can see it, then you would want to secure it with some kind of authentication.

Solution: WordPress has no built-in facility to do it. All you have to do is modify your `.htaccess` file to enable basic HTTP authentication. For that, you have to create the `.htpasswd` file using the `htpasswd` command in Linux. If you are using Windows, then search in Google for `htpasswd.exe` and download it from a reliable location.

Let's create the .htpasswd file by applying this command:

1. Type this command in your command line:

   ```
   htpasswd -cm .htpasswd myusername
   ```

   This `htpasswd` command is a command-line tool available in all Linux distributions by default.

2. Immediately after applying this command, the command-line tool will prompt you for a password; type your password.

 Please note that a `.htpasswd` file containing the encrypted password has been created in the current working folder for the user 'username'.

3. Copy that file to your WordPress folder.

4. The `.htpasswd` file itself is of no use, until you tell Apache what to do with it. So let us create a `.htaccess` file in your WordPress folder with the following content. This content will tell Apache to turn on the basic HTTP authentication using that `.htpasswd` file:

```
AuthType Basic
AuthName "Restricted Area"
AuthUserFile "absolute_url_of_your_.htpasswd_file"
require valid-user
```

Save this file inside your WordPress folder as `.htaccess`. Now whenever you browse this WordPress URL using your browser, it requires the username and password that you created previously.

5. You must supply the absolute URL of the `.htpasswd` file in the `.htaccess` file; it will not work with a relative URL. For example, if your WordPress folder is located inside the `/home/youraccount/public_html/wordpress` folder, then the location of the `.htpasswd` file should be `/home/youraccount/public_html/wordpress/.htpasswd`.

If you have trouble retrieving this absolute path, then please don't worry. Create a PHP file inside this WordPress folder with the following code:

```
<? phpinfo(); ?>
```

Now run this file. You will see a page with a lot of text. Search for the text `_SERVER["DOCUMENT_ROOT"]`, and you will find the absolute URL of this folder on the righthand side of the file. This is how we can modify the `.htpasswd` file to enable HTTP authentication and to make the blog private.

I don't receive the emailed passwords

Problem: You don't receive the emailed passwords.

Cause: This problem may happen if your web server has no **SMTP (Simple Mail Transfer Protocol)** server installed, or if the mail function is explicitly disabled.

Solution: Please contact your system administrator or try installing Sendmail (or any other mail server) properly. It should work.

Tips for theme development

In Chapter 6, we covered theme development pretty thoroughly, though you can get a much more in-depth tutorial in theme development from the excellent book *"WordPress Theme Design"*, *Packt Publishing, 9781847193094*.

This section will clearly list the top template tags and stylesheet classes that you'll want to have if you're going to be developing themes. These are the most essential (with some of my personal favorites thrown in).

Template tags

In the list that follows, I do not cover the arguments that can be passed along with these tags. You'll want to visit the Codex to find out about the default settings for each tag and how to override them.

The **header and informational tags** are as follows:

The tag	What it does
wp_title()	Prints an appropriate title for your blog (the post title, the archives title, the page title, or whatever is appropriate for the current page)
bloginfo('name')	Prints out the name of your blog, as specified on the main options page in your WP Admin
wp_head()	It is an essential part of the <head></head> tag because a variety of things get printed out by this tag, depending on the details of the blog
bloginfo('stylesheet_url')	Prints out the path to the stylesheet for a template
bloginfo('rss2_url')	Prints out the RSS 2.0 feed URL for your blog

These tags that can be used **inside the loop**:

The tag	What it does
the_title()	Prints out the title of the current post or page
the_time()	Prints out the date and time of the post or page
the_content()	Prints out the formatted post or page content
the_category()	Prints out a list of the categories that belong to this post
the_tags()	Prints out a list of the tags associated with this post
the_author()	Prints out the name of the post or page author
edit_post_link()	If the person viewing the blog is a logged-in blog user, this tag will print out a link for editing the post (very handy!)
the_permalink()	Prints out a link to the post or page itself (must be used within a <a href=""></a> tag)

The tag	What it does
comments_popup_link()	If comments_popup_script is not used, this displays a normal link to the comments for the post or page

post_class()	If you put this tag inside the <div> for your posts, it will generate a list of classes for the categories and tags that belong to this post. For example, if you put this in your template:
	
	`<div <?php post_class(); ?>>`
	
	This is what WordPress will create:
	
	`<div class="post category-recipes category-locavore tag-holiday tag-pasta tag-recipe tag-spinach">`

These tags that can be used for **lists and navigation**:

The tag	What it does
prev_post_link()	When viewing a single post, this prints a link to the previous post (the one with the next newest timestamp)
next_post_link()	When viewing a single post, this prints a link to the next post (the one with the next newer timestamp)
wp_list_pages()	Prints a list of all the pages in your WordPress site
wp_get_archives()	Prints a list of archives (by post, by month, and so on)

These tags that can be used to **include** PHP files:

The tag	What it does
get_header()	Includes header.php from the current theme folder
get_footer()	Includes footer.php from the current theme folder
get_sidebar()	Includes sidebar.php from the current theme folder
comments_template()	Prints the standard list of comments and comment-submission form, unless there is a file in the theme folder called comments.php, in which case that is included instead
get_search_form()	Prints the standard search form
include(TEMPLATEPATH. '/filename.php')	Includes filename.php from the current theme folder

Class styles generated by WordPress

WordPress helpfully applies classes to just about everything it generates, thus making it easy for you to style WordPress-generated elements on your page. Here is a starter list of those styles. If you want to know what the other styles are, create a template and view the source of the page it creates.

Class or ID	Where to find it
`.page_item`	On the `<li>` of every page in the generated page list
`.current_page_item`	On the `<li>` of the current page in the generated page list
`.current_page_parent`	On the `<li>` of the parent of the current page in the generated page list
`.page-item-23`	On the `<li>` of the page with ID=23 (there is one of these for each page) in the generated page list
`.widget`	On the `<li>` of every widget
`.cat-item`	On the `<li>` of every category in the generated category list
`.current-cat`	On the `<li>` of the current category in the generated category list
`.cat-item-13`	On the `<li>` of the category with ID=13 (there is one of these for each category) in the generated category list
`#searchform`	On the `<form>` for the generated search form

Learning more

If you want a complete list of template tags, refer to the WordPress Codex at `http://codex.wordpress.org/Template_Tags`.

Summary

In this chapter, we covered many of the common administrative tasks you may face when you're managing a WordPress-driven website. This includes backing up your database and files, moving your WordPress installation from one server or folder to another, and doing general problem-solving and troubleshooting.

We also covered some of the most basic and useful template tags that you'll need when creating your own WordPress themes.

You should now feel well-equipped to address all of the more and less usual administrative tasks for your website or blog.

WordPress is an excellent blogging engine and CMS, which has matured tremendously over the years. The WordPress Admin panel is designed to be user-friendly and is continually being improved. The code that underlies WordPress is robust, and is the creation of a large community of dedicated developers. Additionally, WordPress's functionality can be extended through the use of plugins.

I hope you have enjoyed this book and have gotten a strong start with administering and using WordPress for your own site, whatever it may be. Be sure to stay connected to the WordPress open source community. Happy blogging!

Index

Symbols

A

B

P

Packt Open Source Project Royalties

When we sell a book written on an Open Source project, we pay a royalty directly to that project. Therefore by purchasing WordPress 2.7 Complete, Packt will have given some of the money received to the WordPress project.

In the long term, we see ourselves and you—customers and readers of our books—as part of the Open Source ecosystem, providing sustainable revenue for the projects we publish on. Our aim at Packt is to establish publishing royalties as an essential part of the service and support a business model that sustains Open Source.

If you're working with an Open Source project that you would like us to publish on, and subsequently pay royalties to, please get in touch with us.

Writing for Packt

We welcome all inquiries from people who are interested in authoring. Book proposals should be sent to author@packtpub.com. If your book idea is still at an early stage and you would like to discuss it first before writing a formal book proposal, contact us; one of our commissioning editors will get in touch with you.

We're not just looking for published authors; if you have strong technical skills but no writing experience, our experienced editors can help you develop a writing career, or simply get some additional reward for your expertise.

About Packt Publishing

Packt, pronounced 'packed', published its first book "Mastering phpMyAdmin for Effective MySQL Management" in April 2004 and subsequently continued to specialize in publishing highly focused books on specific technologies and solutions.

Our books and publications share the experiences of your fellow IT professionals in adapting and customizing today's systems, applications, and frameworks. Our solution-based books give you the knowledge and power to customize the software and technologies you're using to get the job done. Packt books are more specific and less general than the IT books you have seen in the past. Our unique business model allows us to bring you more focused information, giving you more of what you need to know, and less of what you don't.

Packt is a modern, yet unique publishing company, which focuses on producing quality, cutting-edge books for communities of developers, administrators, and newbies alike. For more information, please visit our website: www.PacktPub.com.

WordPress for Business Bloggers

ISBN: 978-1-847195-32-6   Paperback: 356 pages

Promote and grow your WordPress blog with advanced plug-ins, analytics, advertising, and SEO

1. Gain a competitive advantage with a well polished WordPress business blog

2. Develop and transform your blog with strategic goals

3. Create your own custom design using the Sandbox theme

4. Apply SEO (search engine optimization) to your blog

5. Market and measure the success of your blog

WordPress 2.7 Cookbook

ISBN: 978-1-847197-38-2   Paperback: 275 pages

100 simple but incredibly useful recipes to take control of your WordPress blog layout, themes, widgets, plug-ins, security, and SEO

1. Take your WordPress blog to the next level with solutions to common WordPress problems that make your blog better, smarter, faster, and more secure

2. Enhance your SEO and make more money online by applying simple hacks

3. Fully tested and compatible with WordPress 2.7

4. Part of Packt's Cookbook series: Each recipe is a carefully organized sequence of instructions to complete the task as efficiently as possible

Please check **www.PacktPub.com** for information on our titles

WordPress Plugin Development: Beginner's Guide

ISBN: 978-1-847193-59-9   Paperback: 296 pages

Build powerful, interactive plug-ins for your blog and to share online

1. Everything you need to create and distribute your own plug-ins following WordPress coding standards

2. Walk through the development of six complete, feature-rich, real-world plug-ins that are being used by thousands of WP users

3. Written by Vladimir Prelovac, WordPress expert and developer of WordPress plug-ins such as Smart YouTube and Plugin Central

4. Part of Packt's Beginners Guide series: expect step-by-step instructions with an emphasis on experimentation and tweaking code

WordPress Theme Design

ISBN: 978-1-847193-09-4   Paperback: 224 pages

A complete guide to creating professional WordPress themes

1. Take control of the look and feel of your WordPress site

2. Simple, clear tutorial to creating Unique and Beautiful themes

3. Expert guidance with practical step-by-step instructions for theme design

4. Design tips, tricks, and troubleshooting ideas

Please check **www.PacktPub.com** for information on our titles

881488

Printed in Great Britain by
Amazon.co.uk, Ltd.,
Marston Gate.